Without a Vision My People Prosper

David Hayward

DEDICATION

To my wife Lisa, who knows exactly what I mean.

CONTENTS

ACKNOWLEDGMENTS

I am thankful to all the churches I have been a part of. Without my long experience and my years of ministry within the church, I would not have been able to write what I wrote within these pages. I especially am grateful to Rothesay Vineyard Christian Fellowship in New Brunswick, Canada, the last local church I was a pastor of, for giving me the experience of true community.

Introduction

Here follows a collection of my posts from my blog, nakepastor.com, on the topic of vision. I decided to compile these short posts because they drew so much interest and debate on my blog. Rather than organize an extended essay or series of chapters on the issue, the posts seem to have expressed the essence of my argument. Why reinvent the wheel?

So what we have here is like a quilt. My hope is that, no matter how crazy this quilt is, the pieces still somehow sew together to make a completed whole. Even though no single post will drive home my point, I certainly trust that the entire collection will.

I want to emphasize in this short introduction that I apply my argument to church communities. I do not address businesses or other organizations, institutions or social clubs. Nor do I apply this argument necessarily to individual people. My case is that church community is a different creature from these other ones, and that this needs to be respected and protected. As you will see, I frequently compare church community to family. This runs into problems of its own, mainly because family is hard to define anymore. But, alas, I'm starting to repeat what my posts have already said.

I've included many of my own cartoons that address the issue of vision in the church as well. I hope you enjoy them.

My cover illustration was inspired by Picasso's "Don Quixote", the story of a man overcome by fantasy.

Disillusionment (May 19, 2006)

> *Innumerable times a whole Christian community has broken down because it has sprung from a wish dream.*

The serious Christian, set down for the first time in a Christian community, is likely to bring with him a very definite idea of what Christian life together should be and try to realize it. But God's grace speedily shatters such dreams. Just as surely as God desires to lead us to a knowledge of genuine Christian fellowship, so surely must we be overwhelmed by a great disillusionment with others, with Christians in general, and, if we are fortunate, with ourselves (Bonhoeffer, *Life Together*).

The power of the truth of this statement is frightening, especially for anyone who has designs for a church. That would be me, as well as most other pastors and keen Christians. As I wrote yesterday, God graciously frustrates these designs. Bonhoeffer goes on to insist that God will not allow us to live even for a moment in a dream world. But it seems to be the fad of the day to live in a dream world when it comes to our Christianity and our churches. We honestly think we can change a group of people overnight or over time into something we want them to be! If God does shatter these dreams, I think it is just as necessary that we be sensitive, somehow, to this shattering… open to it, invite it, embrace it. Because to live in the dream world prevents us from living in *this* world of reality with the actual people around us.

As a pastor, I constantly ask the question: Is there a way we can just be a fellowship of believers and put away our dreams and visions which really are expectations, which quickly translates into coercion? Is there a way? Can all who will, gather in simple fellowship?

Bonhoeffer continues:

"Only that fellowship which faces such disillusionment with all its unhappy and ugly aspects, begins to be what it should be in God's sight, begins to grasp in faith the promise that is given to it. The sooner this shock of disillusionment comes to an individual and to a community

the better for both. A community that cannot bear and cannot survive such a crisis, which insists upon keeping its illusion when it should be shattered, permanently loses in that moment the promise of Christian community. Sooner or later it will collapse. Every human wish dream that is injected into the Christian community is a hindrance to genuine community and must be banished if genuine community is to survive. He who loves his dream of a community more than the Christian community itself becomes a destroyer of the latter, even though his personal intentions may be ever so honest and earnest and sacrificial.”

My church went through a split in 1997. I know what it means to be shattered. We still live. We are survivors. I often wonder how much of the split was caused by illusions and dreams applied to the fellowship that it just couldn't live up to or bear. Since then, we have tried so hard to live humbly and simply as a community, without complication, without illusion, without manipulation or coercion. I want to tell you: it is nearly impossible. In fact, I would say it is virtually humanly impossible as a Christian fellowship to live up to Bonhoeffer's insight. But we try, firmly believing that this is right and the best, even perfect, way, of being a Christian fellowship. It is the most humane and liberating for people. It is beautiful when it is given and experienced.

Nouwen, the Wounded Prophet, and the Church (May 22, 2006)

I've been thinking about ministry and what it means to be a pastor. I keep asking myself the question: is it possible for all kinds of different people to dwell together in unity? That is, can a particular local church be made up of a wide variety of people, and yet be united? Can there be true unity in vast diversity? I'm not just talking about diversity in appearance or superficial issues, but diversity in beliefs, theology, orientations and lifestyles. I work hard. Sometimes I lose hope, but sometimes I see glimpses.

I'm reminded of a book I read a few years back by Michael Ford, *Wounded Prophet*. It is his biographical account of Henri Nouwen, a prominent Roman Catholic priest who taught Spiritual Theology and mysticism at Harvard, then ended up being a worker alongside Jean Vanier at a L'Arche community in Richmond Hill, ON, Canada. He died a few years ago, leaving behind him several books on spirituality and prayer. He touched many lives around the world, including mine in a significant way. In this book, he tells us about a time when Nouwen went on retreat to some friends in the country, and he began to just meet in the red barn on their property to pray and celebrate mass. A friend joined him, then another friend, then another… until there was quite a number of people meeting with him. This is his account:

At Nouwen's sabbatical in the Red Barn Community, he comments:

> *Ministry happens. I have done nothing here while on sabbatical to do ministry. I didn't come here to get people who mostly don't go to church to join me in prayer and the Eucharist. I just started to pray, and invited one person to join me, and these others' neighbors and friends simply came. I'm not concerned with fixing the marriage of the one who is considering divorce or convincing the woman who doesn't believe in Jesus. I'm here to say this is who I am, and to be there for others* (Michael Ford, *Wounded Prophet*).

With his own struggles in mind, Nouwen could only ask himself the obvious question: "Who am I to judge?" When I read this my heart said, Yes! Is there a way, like this community, that we can all just gather with all our problems and issues and differing theologies and lifestyles without trying to fix each other? Is there a way we can serve each other without the ulterior motive of trying to change the ones we serve? Is there a way we can truly love each other without caution or reserve?

These, I feel, are significant questions that need to be asked if we have any concern at all for the future of the church, spiritual communities, or any community for that matter.

Leadership and Wealth (May 23, 2006)

In Elie Wiesel's book, *Night*, he relates a story of a man called Moishe. They would have theological discussions now and then. Moishe asked Elie who he prayed to and why. Elie asked Moishe the same question in return. Moishe said, "*I pray to the God within me for the strength to ask Him the real questions*"

7

(p. 5). Yes, the courage to ask the real questions!

So, I'm just asking questions… questions that have haunted me for years and years. Here's something that directly applies to the ministry and church life. Read this and ask, *"How does this fly in the face of popular religion today?"*

> *"The desire we so often hear expressed today for 'episcopal figures', 'priestly men', 'authoritative personalities' springs frequently enough from a spiritually sick need for the admiration of men, for the establishment of visible human authority, because the genuine authority of service appears to be so unimpressive"* (Bonhoeffer, *Life Together*).

Leadership is a hot topic today. Everyone's reading about it. Me too. But I'm having problems with what I'm reading. I agree with it on one level, but then my mind *immediately* asks the question: But does this apply to pastoral ministry? Does it apply to the church? I'm serious! Does it? To put Jesus' statement in question form, *"If the kings of the Gentiles lord it over them, is this how you are to behave?"* What's most interesting is that this comment of Jesus is in reaction to the disciples: *"A dispute also arose among them as to which one of them was to be regarded as the greatest"* (*Mark* 22: 24f). Dynamic and deserved leadership was the rule back then too.

Look at this:

> *"Leaders have always played a primordial emotional role. No doubt humankind's original leaders- whether tribal chieftans or shamanesses- earned their place in large part because their leadership was emotionally compelling. Throughout history and in cultures everywhere, the leader in any human group has been the one to whom others look for assurance and clarity when faces uncertainty or threat, or when there's a job to be done. The leader acts as the group's emotional guide"* (Goleman, Boyatzis, McKee, *Primal Leadership: Learning to Lead with Emotional Intelligence*).

I have no doubt this is correct, but for some reason I don't think it always should apply to spiritual leadership. The Old Testament intimates when God conceded and granted Israel's demand for a king like other nations, that this lead to innumerable woes. Moses was not a natural leader, and he knew it. Jeremiah, the weeping prophet, now there's emotional assurance! Paul: emotionally compelling? Jesus? How did Jesus' emotions fair in the field of *"talent retention"* (*Primal Leadership*)?

Another field that has incredible popularity these days is money and wealth. Book after book is being published and read. I read them too. But even though I agree with what they say, I have a very hard time applying their principals to my life. In his book, *Five Lessons a Millionaire Taught Me*, Evans claims, even before you hit lesson number one, is that I have to decide *right now*, before I read on, that I want *more than anything else* to be a millionaire. Same with T. Harv Eker's book, *Secrets of a Millionaire Mind*: before I go any further, I must decide that becoming wealthy is my number one priority! I can understand that. But I have a huge problem jumping over this first hurdle to enter that race. Do I want wealth acquisition to be my first priority?

What kind of church did Bonhoeffer describe with the kind of leadership he wrote about? The pressure to be a charismatic, influential, contagious, and attractive leader is irresistible today. But it seems that if you want the kind of church that is most desirable today, you have to agree to play by its rules of leadership. Like the books I mentioned on wealth: am I willing to jump over that first hurdle in order to enter that kind of race? Am I willing to be the kind of leader so promoted today in order to get the kind of church so proudly paraded today?

Faith Ain't Always Sweet (May 24, 2006)

I read Oswald Chamber's *My Utmost For His Highest* this morning, as I do most mornings. I love the sheer honesty of his insights. In today's entry he comments on *Revelation* 1:17: *"And when I saw Him, I fell at his feet as dead."*

> *"It may be that like the apostle John you know Jesus Christ intimately, when suddenly He appears with no familiar characteristic at all, and the only thing you can do is to fall at His feet as dead. There are times when God cannot reveal Himself in any other way than in His majesty, and it is the awfulness of the vision which brings you to the delight of despair; if you are ever to be raised up, it must be by the hand of God."*

This reminds me of a prayer of Thomas Merton's:

> *"Dear God, I have no idea where I'm going. I do not see the road ahead of me. I cannot know for certain where it will end. Nor do I really know myself: and the fact that I think that I am following you will does not mean that I am actually doing so. But I believe this: I believe that the desire to please you does in fact please you. I hope I have that desire in everything I do. I hope I never persist in anything apart from that desire. And I know that if I do this, You will lead me by the right road, though I may know nothing about it at the time. In the 'shadow of death' I will not be afraid, because I know You will never leave me to face my troubles all alone."*

I do believe that during the times of greatest confusion, that they may actually be times of greatest revelation. I think Luther stated that confusion and faith are closely related. In fact, I think he said certainty and faith are opposites, enemies of each other!

Here's Barth:

> *"Just as surely as the recognition of the sovereignty of God overthrows all confidence in human righteousness, it sets erect no other ground of confidence. Men are not deprived of one security, in order that they may immediately discover for themselves another. No man can shelter himself behind the triumphant will of God; rather, when it is once perceived, he comes under judgment and enters into a condition of shattering confusion from which he can never escape: neither forwards nor backwards can we escape from this narrow gorge. There is therefore no alternative for us but to remain under the indictment; and only he who remains here without making any attempts to escape, even by spinning sophistries of human logic: is able to praise God in His faithfulness:"* (Barth, *Romans*).

11

Welcome to the deep struggles of faith! (*Above is one of my images of Karl Barth. Pen and ink on paper.*)

Love and Church Membership (May 26, 2006)

Read this passage from N. T. Wright's, *What Saint Paul Really Said*:

> *"A brief word about love. Paul does not mean that all Christians should feel warm fuzzy feelings for each other. That romantic and existentialist reading of agape does not begin to capture what is really going on. The critical thing is that the church, those who worship God in Christ Jesus, should function as a family in which every member is accepted as an equal member, no matter what their social, cultural or moral background. The very existence of such a community demonstrates to the principalities and powers, the hidden but powerful forces of prejudice and suspicion, that their time is up, that the living God has indeed won*

the victory over them, that there is now launched upon the world a different way of being human, a way in which the traditional distinctions between human beings are done away with. That is why we find in Ephesians the climactic statement: the purpose of the gospel is that 'through the church the manifold wisdom of God might be made known to the principalities and powers in the heavenly places' (Ephesians 3:10). The very existence of a community of love, love where before there was mutual suspicion and distrust, is the crucial piece of evidence that tells Paul that God's spirit has been at work (Colossians 1:8)".

True unity, the kind of unity that can only be made manifest in the climate of Wright's statement above, does not necessarily feel warm and fuzzy. True unity is something that has already been accomplished in the cross of Christ (Ephesians 2: 14), and continually sustained by the Spirit. Our assignment, if we choose to accept it, is to practice it (Ephesians 4:3). I've experienced division in the church, and some of it quite ugly. What usually follows is pressure from well-wishers to restore the warm, fuzzy feelings that were obviously lost. I've never felt that was necessary because I'm certain that the truest unity at the deepest level wasn't severed. It is true that "mutual suspicion", "distrust", and "prejudice" need to be fought against. What I've discovered is that the spirit of distrust, prejudice, and suspicion prospers in the church more than anywhere else, because many believe that the church is THE place where people are categorized according to their morals, ideologies, theologies, lifestyles, opinions, and so on. The church quickly becomes a place where people are distinguished from each other, often with judgment following close on its heels.

This topic gets tricky because the Spirit challenges us to practice unity. Do we practice unity with those who practice disunity? Do we practice unconditional love with those who love conditionally? Do we practice trust with people who distrust others? The bible says have nothing to do with a divisive person. Often that is translated to mean anyone who tries to overthrow a pastor or break up a congregation. But I now believe a divisive person is anyone who excludes people based on their differences. The catch-22: do we exclude exclusivists?

Wright continues later in the book:

> "(we must tell them), in the name of Jesus, that there is a different way of being human, a way characterized by self-giving love, by justice, by honesty, and by the breaking down of the traditional barriers that reinforce the divisions which keep human beings separate from, and as often as not at odds with, one another. And, of course, it is no good saying all this if the church is not saying it by its very life. As I shall suggest presently, this message is at its most powerful when it is presented in symbols and praxis,

not merely in dogma and story".

He writes later:

> "*Any attempt to define church membership by any other than allegiance to Jesus Christ is, quite simply, idolatrous: It is by the church living as the one believing community, in which barriers of race, class, gender and so forth are irrelevant to membership and to holding office, that the principalities and powers are informed in no uncertain terms that their time is up, that there is indeed a new way of being human*".

So, here at my home church, we probably err on the side of trying to practice unconditional love. What more can be said? What more can be done?

The Limited Mind (June 6, 2006)

Unless we radically change the way we do or are the church, we are in trouble. We are doomed to the endless cycle of human invention, even if it is ingenious. The problem is that we only think inside the box. It is the mind's predicament to limit itself to the only categories it knows. It collects what the eyes see and the ears hear to assemble thoughts. The mind can only conceive of things it creates with the raw matter it receives. It can only construct with the materials it is given. Our minds have taken years building its arsenal of materials, components, and parts. The mind's thoughts have accumulated over time, and we are at least reluctant, if not vehemently opposed to, not using these accumulated materials to build our vision of what should be next. It is repugnant to and impossible for our minds to consider that it doesn't have the parts to conceive the next step.

What if we for a moment truly leaned *not* on our own understanding, and put the mind at rest? What if we stopped our brains from working in their normal patterns? What if we considered that the answer lies beyond our thoughts, beyond our intelligence, beyond human wisdom? Are we finally tired of strategizing, brain-storming, envisioning, concocting, futuring, and paradigming? I am! What about waiting? What about calming ourselves, stilling our minds, and simply allowing what has been prepared for us to be birthed in our midst?

I for one believe that this is not only a more biblical posture, but "*all spirituality and religion aside*" a more humane one.

"*No eye has seen, no ear has heard, no mind has conceived what God has prepared for those who love him*" (1 Corinthians 2:9).

Leadership and Mountain Climbing (June 7, 2006)

Isaiah, the Old Testament prophet, reports a promise of God: "*I will lead the blind by ways they have not known, along unfamiliar paths I will guide them*" (42: 14-16).

Can we take this seriously? Is it possible to follow paradigms no longer, old or new, borrowed from other institutions, books, or leaders, but to become truly innovative and creative in the way God is: *ex nihilo* (from nothing!), to cross all boundaries and stretch wide the corners of our tents and cross new frontiers and boldly go where no one has gone before?

I'm challenging all! It demands enormous courage. Incredible risks must be taken. But we will be guided one step at a time, if only we accept our blindness. It is a frightening way to lead because we always plot out where we'd like to go, or where we are actually going. We like to be and appear precocious, visionary and organized. This is how we've always done it, and where has it gotten us? We have only renovated the old and created recycled paradigms. True leadership means one day at a time. It appears haphazard and messy, but this is what it is like to walk blindly along unfamiliar paths.

If we live by the Spirit, let us keep in step with the Spirit (Galatians 5: 25). This is a new paradigm that isn't a paradigm. It demands tight relationship with the Spirit. But it also demands a tight relationship with the leadership. There has to be trust, longsuffering, and patience. It is high-risk, and probably too high risk for investors. It is like mountain climbing on a mountain face you've never been on. You have no idea where the next spike will go until you are right upon it. You can plot your general direction: "Up!" but that's about all the pre-planning you can do. What it takes is self-preparation more than anything. Are we ready to make such an ascent?

Art of the Start (June 28, 2006)

Here's an excellent statement:

"Innovation often originates outside the existing organizations, in part because successful organizations acquire a commitment to the status quo and a resistance to ideas that might change it" (Nathan Rosenburg, quoted in Guy Kawasaki, *The Art of the Start*).

This is one of the issues of any institution, including the church. I read lots of material on the desperate need for innovative thinking to change the church. It is desperate for all the obvious reasons that I won't get into right now. The problem is that most of this material is written from within the institution by people like me... paid professionals.

Which is why the desert is such a strong and important symbol in scripture and throughout the history of the church. If we want to critique the church and be innovative, we *must* go to the desert first.

Wendell Berry, the American social critic, has something to say about this in his book, *The Unsettling of America*. Berry believes the pursuit of truth is better than the protection of truth. Once the mind has "*consented to be orthodox*", then it becomes "*narrow, rigid, mercenary, morally corrupt, and vengeful against dissenters.*" He says this is the nature of

@nakedpastor

"Just remember guys: you are doing this for God, not for me!"

orthodoxy: *"one who presumes to know the truth does not look for it"*. He draws a direct analogy from religion:

> *"The pattern of orthodoxy in religion, because it is well known, gives us a useful paradigm. The encrusted religious structure is not changed by its institutional dependents– they are part of the crust. It is changed by one who goes alone to the wilderness, where he fasts and prays, and returns with cleansed vision. In going alone, he goes independent of institutions, forswearing orthodoxy ('right opinion'). In going to the wilderness he goes to the margin, where he is surrounded by the possibilities– by no means all good– that orthodoxy has excluded. By fasting he disengages his thoughts from the immediate issues of livelihood; his willing hunger takes his mind off the payroll, so to speak. And by praying he acknowledges ignorance;*

the orthodox presume to know, whereas the marginal person is trying to find out. He returns to the community not necessarily with new truth, but with a new vision of the truth he see it more whole than before".

Let's go to the desert! Or maybe recognize that we are already there and take advantage of it.

Are Goals, Destinations and Alternatives Burdens? (June 20, 2006)

This post is in response to a few comments made on some previous posts. Comments like I am a church-basher, a cynic, overwhelmingly negative, and a deconstructionist. I am very, very grateful for the variety of comments being made, and I invite more.

Here's an apology in my defense: I decided long ago that the problem with the church isn't finding a way forward or alternatives or revisions or renovations. In my opinion, the church doesn't need a destination, a goal, or a way forward, any more than a family does! I decided that my ministry is about the removal of all these obstacles. Jesus was highly critical of those who kept heaping more and more expectations, laws, requirements, mores, and guilt upon people. He saw them as harmful burdens. He invited people to follow him because his burden was light. So, I am convinced that my ministry's mandate is to strip people of all burdens, and to pare the church down to practically nothing. It looks like church-bashing and deconstruction because we tend to equate all the unnecessary extras with the church.

If you want to read a man who was a severe critic of the church while being a committed part of it, read William Stringfellow's *An Ethic For Christians and Other Aliens in a Strange Land*.

I believe in the gift of absolute liberty of the human being, and the real fellowship we all share in Christ. That's the church.

Simple as that!

A Response to a Response, and Lincoln (June 20, 2006)

Thanks John for your thoughtful comment on today's earlier blog. On our way to Kansas City for the conference I wrote about in yesterday's blog: I bought the book Lincoln by David Herbert Donald. When I read the following passage, it timely

grooved with the insight I received upon hearing from the Cambodian pastor:

"From his earliest days Lincoln had a sense that his destiny was controlled by some larger force, some Higher Power. Turning away from orthodox Christianity because of the emotional excesses of frontier evangelism, he found it easier as a young man to accept what was called the Doctrine of Necessity, which he defined as the belief 'that the human mind is impelled to action, or held in rest by some power, over which the mind itself has no control.' Later, he frequently quoted to his partner, William H. Herndon, the lines for Hamlet: 'There's a divinity that shapes our ends, rough-hew them how he will.'" From Lincoln's fatalism derived some of his most lovable traits: his compassion, his tolerance, his willingness to overlook mistakes. That belief did not, of course, lend him to lethargy or dissipation. Like thousands of Calvinists who believed in predestination, he worked indefatigably for a better world for himself, for his family, and for his nation. But it helped to buffer the many reverses that he experienced and enabled him to continue a strenuous life of aspiration. "It also made for a pragmatic approach to problems, a recognition that if one solution as fated not to work another could be tried. 'My policy is to have no policy' became a kind of motto from Lincoln… a motto that infuriated the sober, doctrinaire people around him who were inclined to think that the President had no principals either. He might have offended his critics less if he had more often used the analogy he gave James G. Blaine when explaining his course on Reconstruction: 'The pilots on our Western rivers steer from point to point as they call it: 'setting the course of the boat no further than they can see; and that is all I propose to myself in this great problem.'

"Both statements suggest Lincoln's reluctance to take the initiative and make bold plans; he preferred to respond to the actions of others. They also show why Lincoln in his own distinctively American way had the quality John Keats

defined as forming ' a Man of Achievement', that quality 'which Shakespeare possessed so enormously: Negative Capability, that is when a man is capable of being in uncertainties, Mysteries, doubts, without any irritable reaching after fact and reason'".

I question our modern fascination with visions and goals and strategies to get there, especially when it comes to the individual and to the church.

How to Build an Independent Bookstore (August 7, 2006)

This is in response to some comments concerning my recent post that said, "*all truth is God's truth*". Listen to this account of Warren Farka, founder of the eccentrically funky 8th Day Books:

> "*We hope there is a coherence within this eccentric community of books, an organizing principal of selection: if a book, be it literary, scientific, historical, or theological, sheds light on ultimate questions in an excellent way, then it's a worthy candidate for inclusion in this catalogue. Reality doesn't divide itself into 'religious' or 'literary' or 'secular' spheres, so we don't either; we are convinced that all truths are related, and every truth, if we pay attention rightly, directs our gaze toward God. One of our customers found us 'eclectic but orthodox'. We like that. We also resonate with Saint Justin Martyr in his Second Apology (paraphrased a bit): that which is true is ours*" (*Image, A Journal of the Arts and Religion*: "That Which is True is Ours: How to Build an Independent Bookstore").

I wrote this quote into my journal over a year ago because I so identified with it and hopefully envisioned this as a possible description of our church: '*eclectic but orthodox*'. You see, I feel it is entirely possible for me to, like Paul, make central to my preaching that "*in Christ God was reconciling the world to himself*" (2 Corinthians 5:19) while at the same time

©nakedpastor

encouraging and exemplifying diversity in the community (that's the orthodoxy with eclecticism). So, even though I, as a pastor, am working among people, not books, I share Farka's perspective.

I Feel Like We're Changing (September 12, 2006)

I feel like my church is changing. It used to be a tight fellowship. The whole church had a commune feel to it. If you were a part of the church, it had an all-or-nothing aura about it. If you signed up, you were signing up for 100% commitment. There are pros and cons to this. One pro was those involved were very committed, making for incredible energy and vision. A con was that it tended to stratify people into different levels of commitment. In a nutshell, it used to be that a system was imposed upon the people. The leadership's expectations were laid upon the people as to how they were to develop spiritually.

Now, we basically have Sunday morning gathering where worship opportunities are provided, studying the Bible is provided, and prayer is provided. We also provide this for children. That's it! If people want more, it is available, such as small-groups. But it is not imposed. Only provided. Basically, there are three stages of growth opportunities provided: general (Sunday mornings); basic (study groups, task groups, small groups, and impromptu fellowships); and focused (one on one spiritual direction and counseling for those who request it). But anyone can grow with or without any of these. These are only available provisions we feel are in keeping with human liberty and rights.

I make it sound like we have it all down. We don't. I'm basically guessing. I'm not describing it well. But the inability to label it is part of the paradigm because it is no longer about a *prescription for processing people*. It's now about providing room, inclusion, and opportunity for people to process *themselves* in cooperation with the Spirit. It used to feel tight. Now it feels loose. If I were a control-freak (and I have been accused of that), I could be freaking out about this. But I'm not. Space, room, freedom and choice are my tag words now.

Leaders or Elders (March 7, 2007)

I've been thinking lots lately about terminology. For years our community has used the term "leader", "leadership", and "leadership team". These terms do not belong in a community such as this anymore. "Leadership" gives the impression of directing others, telling them how to behave, someone in front of all the others, and that there is a goal to be strived for and conquered. It conjures up images of ambition, competition, manipulation, coercion, exploitation and success. It breeds discontentment for the present reality. It is based on a business model of people-management and is so strongly goal-oriented that it damages the beauty of what is. Love, in this milieu, is in danger of being used as a commodity to achieve the wishes of the visionary leader.

I'm now thinking that we need to return to the word "elder". It is old-fashioned, I know, but I think it better describes

what community is about. "Elder" is not so much about movement outward towards a goal, but is more about growth and maturity. It is about responsibility, service and care. It is about acknowledging the hard-earned wisdom of someone who has a natural influence among the people that isn't fabricated or artificial, but tangible and practiced. There is less danger of using people to achieve ends. Rather, people are respected as the end in themselves. Love, rather than a means to an end, becomes the end itself. These are my thoughts at the moment.

And the Winner Is (March 12, 2007)

I must say I didn't expect the response I received from the

"Wow! That's a huge vision you have for your people!"

post on leadership. Over 150 comments! I really appreciated all the comments.

I want to emphasize that I really don't care about titles at all. They are just labels. But we all must admit that labels and titles must necessarily point to a reality. The word isn't the thing, but they certainly can point to the thing. What I am searching for is a way to do community that isn't burdensome to people, but in fact is an expression of freedom and love. Although I think our community is on to something, I think we still have a ways to go. If there is any slight sniff of coercion, control, manipulation, expectation, judgment or condemnation in a community, then something is terribly wrong. I am highly suspicious of vision-casting, goal-setting or being purpose-driven. You may think I am reactionary, but I don't think I am. I agree with Bonhoeffer, who said that *"God hates visionary dreaming"*! Why? Because it hates and destroys the community that already exits as it is. *"When the morning mists of dreams vanish, then dawns the bright day of… fellowship"* (Bonhoeffer).

Not Easy Being Me (April 5, 2007)

One of the most difficult things for anyone to be is him- or herself. It takes a lifetime of hard work and courage to discover who we are and to settle down to be that person. And that's if we are willing. As Carl Jung once wrote: *"Live your life or be dragged!"*

I encourage people to be authentically themselves. You might think that this would be a wonderful idea that would attract people because we assume people love authenticity. We don't. We prefer pretense and masks, not only in ourselves, but also in others. Authenticity is very ugly and chaotic before it gets beautiful and serene. I know, because I see this in my own life and in the life of our community. The first step, being authentic ourselves, is the first hurtle that most people don't clear. The next hurtle is appreciating authenticity in others. That's where the rest opt out.

This doesn't only apply to the people out there, but to me also, the pastor. I try to be authentically me. When I first made this dangerous decision about 10 years ago, I think this was one thing that contributed to the church split that nearly leveled our church. But I wouldn't go back, even for job-security. I read this in Barth years ago that applies:

> *It is as the persons they are that preachers are called to this task, as these specific people with their own characteristics and histories. It is as the persons they are that they have been selected and called. This is what is meant by originality. Pastors are not to adopt a role. They are not to slip into the clothing of biblical characters. That would be the worst kind of comedy. They are not to be Luthers, churchmen, prophets, visionaries, or the like. They are simply to be themselves, and to expound the text as such. Preaching is the responsible word of a person of our own time. Having heard myself, I am called upon to pass on what I have heard. Even as ministers, it matters that these persons be what they are. They must not put on a character or a robe. They do not have to play a role. It is*

you who have been commissioned, you, just as you are, not as minister, as pastor or theologian, not under any concealment or cover, but you yourself have simply to discharge this commission.

My Vision is to Have No Vision (May 14, 2007)

I went to another Vineyard leaders meeting this last weekend. I love the people. That's the only reason I go, to be honest. I get so tired of the ceaseless talk about vision, vision forming, vision casting, vision keeping, blah, blah, blah. I am against vision. Call me an idiot! I don't care. I told everyone in my small group, after all the talk about vision, that I personally resist vision with as much passion as those who believe in it. I get the usual quote: *"Without a vision, the people perish."* I don't believe it. Today, people perish with vision. Besides, the original language of that passage (Proverbs 29: 18) doesn't mean "vision" as in a corporate long-term goal. It means "revelation". In other words, without hearing from God, the people perish. It is truth we need. Not another vision, *please*!

I've created and tried to sustain vision in the past, as well as press its importance on the church. And I've seen those visions crush people and myself, especially when the vision is withered up and proven empty. Some people say, *"Well, then get a better vision!"* No! I learned my lesson right away: vision kills. I refuse to try to create vision or vision-cast or get the community to shape one and pursue it. Why? Because it kills what is. It murders life.

When asked what our vision is as a church, I said we don't have one and will not have one. We simply get together to worship, fellowship, gather around the bible, help those who need it. That's it. *"Well then that's your vision!"* Don't try to squeeze me into your box just so you will be comfortable with me! I don't have a vision. Our community doesn't have a vision. We don't have a mission statement. As a father of a family, I don't have any vision other than that we love one another. I don't set any long-term goals as a father of my children or as a husband of my wife. Simply love. To set goals for my family would be demonic.

I know this sounds brutal to some, but brutality against

bondage to anything, even vision, is necessary today. Vision is used to escape the present and to destroy what is. I won't have it. I've tasted and seen that it is bad. My goal is to have no goal. My vision is visionless. I be. We be. That's it.

My Vision is to Have No Vision: Part 2 (May 15, 2007)

I had no idea yesterday's post would stir up so much controversy. And even though this blog is a place for me to express my personal opinion, I have to admit that I do believe that this view of "vision" would be best for all. It was Bonhoeffer, not the nakedpastor, who said, "*God hates visionary dreaming*"! Why? Because it hates and destroys the

community that already exits as it is. He said, "*When the morning mists of dreams vanish, then dawns the bright day of fellowship.*" He continues:

> *Innumerable times a whole Christian community has broken down because it has sprung from a wish dream. The serious Christian, set down for the first time in a Christian community, is likely to bring with him a very definite idea of what Christian life together should be and try to realize it. But God's grace speedily shatters such dreams. Just as surely as God desires to lead us to a knowledge of genuine*

Christian fellowship, so surely must we be overwhelmed be a great disillusionment with others, with Christians in general, and, if we are fortunate, with ourselves.

And again:

Every human wish dream that is injected into the Christian community is a hindrance to genuine community and must be banished if genuine community is to survive. He who loves his dream of a community more than the Christian community itself becomes a destroyer of the latter, even though his personal intentions may be ever so honest and earnest and sacrificial.

When will we learn? It is time for huge and universal change. I'm not just tired of vision and mission and goals. I've come to conclude that universally for the church these are deadly to what is and an affront to grace! The philosopher Krishnamurti said,

The feeling that one must be something is the beginning of deception, and, of course, this idealistic attitude leads to various forms of hypocrisy.

Time to stop dreaming and get down to who we are. That is enough. We've been practicing this, and if you need to know...

it does work! But even saying that is a defiling of it. As Luther once said, *"Put two lovers in a bedroom together... you won't have to tell them what to do!"* Are all our strategies, mission statements, vision-casting, and goal-setting are a psycho-sexual avoidance of truth and reality.

10 Questions for Religious Leaders (May 17, 2007)

1. Is it possible for people to gather without there being an agenda? In other words, can people gather without feeling that they need to "go" somewhere as a group?
2. Is it possible for people to enjoy the community without having a vision statement?
3. Is it possible for people to stay in community with each other without a set of rules to follow?
4. Is it possible for a community to be composed of people of all kinds of levels of faith and even of no faith at all, or for those who hold vastly differing views of scripture to keep fellowship?
5. Is it possible for people simply to gather without a goal that they must agree to?
6. Is it possible for a community to exist without being controlled by leadership?
7. Is it possible for a person to be a welcomed and appreciated part of the community who disagrees strongly with the pastor or leader on some major issues?
8. Is it possible for people from all across the cultural, social and moral spectrum to love each other face to face in community?
9. Is it possible for a pastor, priest, minister, leader, Imam, master, or whatever, to "allow" a wide and opposing variety of opinions even though he or she may strongly hold his or her own and teach it?
10. Is it possible for a healthy community to exist long-term and to thrive in good works without a mission statement, a vision, or a goal?

Go or Get Dragged! (May 24, 2007)

Prepare for the desert! Hitchens makes a strong statement in his book God is Not Dead:

> To 'choose' dogma and faith over doubt and experiment is to throw out the ripening vintage and to reach greedily for the Kool-Aid.

Which reminded me of something that Wendell Berry wrote in his book, *The Unsettling of America*. Berry believes the pursuit of truth is better than the protection of it. Once the mind has *"consented to be orthodox"*, then it becomes *"narrow, rigid, mercenary, morally corrupt, and vengeful against dissenters."* He says this is the nature of orthodoxy: *"one who presumes to know the truth does not look for it*". He continues:

> *The pattern of orthodoxy in religion, because it is well known, gives us a useful paradigm. The encrusted religious structure is not changed by its institutional dependents... they are part of the crust. It is changed by one who goes alone to the wilderness, where he fasts and prays, and returns with cleansed vision. In going alone, he goes independent of institutions, forswearing orthodoxy ('right opinion'). In going to the wilderness he goes to the margin, where he is surrounded by the possibilities... by no means all good... that orthodoxy has excluded. By fasting he disengages his thoughts from the immediate issues of livelihood; his willing hunger takes his mind off the payroll, so to speak. And by praying he acknowledges ignorance; the orthodox presume to know, whereas the marginal person is trying to find out. He returns to the community not necessarily with new truth, but with a new vision of the truth he see it more whole than before.*

All religions and their adherents need to prepare themselves to enter into this very desert now, to admit that we do not "know" and finally embrace doubt and mystery. I think we must initiate this willingly and humbly because we are going to be dragged there otherwise.

A Business Without a Vision Statement (May 28, 2007)

I spoke with a very successful businessman the other day. He makes millions. He is a spiritual man, a Christian, and we talked about living in the moment, being free of the shame of the past and free of the fear of the future. So I asked him, "*How do you, a business man, take literally Jesus' saying, 'Take no thought for tomorrow'?*" He said that he's thought a great deal about that and decided that when he implements integrity, wisdom and work into all that he does presently, it usually if not always is rewarded with success. So, in a sense, he doesn't have a "vision" for his company. He just does what he does well and with integrity. Literally, when the present is lived authentically, tomorrow does take care of itself. In fact, he says vision has placed a limiting restraint on his success in the past, as well as rendered the work environment artificial, so he canned vision statements. His company is healthier.

Another Visionless Rant (May 30, 2007)

I want to rant! I need to say something right here right now. Just the *thought* of having to sit in a meeting to talk about what we *ought* to do, *should* do, or *must* do, just makes me want to hurl. Just the thought of sitting listening to someone reiterate the vision and try to fire me up to follow it makes me want to quit even before I join. I absolutely love the saying of Jesus, *"Come to me all you who are weary and heavy laden and I will give you rest!"* I'm telling you people: this world is full of people weary and heavy laden with the expectations of religion and its leaders. That's what Jesus was talking about. When he saw the people so burdened and vexed without a shepherd, that's what he was talking about. When he chastised the religious leaders for laying burdens on people without lifting a finger to help them, that's what he was talking about. No amount of our talented tweaking is going to change the weight of the burden, only it's appearance. Let the visions and agendas go! They are only burdensome expectations in modern fancy dress.

I live with teenagers and their friends. Our house is often full of them… loud, funny, wild, uncontrollable, disobedient and visionless. All they want to do is hang. That's it. That is life's pleasure for them. And it is enough. What can be better than being together, loving each other, challenging each other to be more authentic, and laughing? What can be better? Save the world? From what? They'll tell you, *"Let's save the world from control-freaks who are trying to shape us into something other than what we are!"* *"Do not sell your soul to any agenda for any price!"* They're rubbing off on us, and it ain't all bad! What can be better for Lisa and me than to be among these lunatics, laughing with them, teasing them, affirming them in their beauty and aimlessness, and receiving their reckless affection? Answer me that!

Love, a Rose, and a Pastor (June 6, 2007)

I want to make a few things clear:

1. I love my church.
2. I feel called to be a pastor.
3. I want to pastor this church.
4. I am grateful to be her pastor.

Methinks I don't protest too much. Let me put it this way: it is as though I came across an extraordinarily beautiful rose in the wilderness. My task is to appreciate, protect and praise its rare beauty. Along come the developers to suggest digging up this rose's roots in order to plant a whole garden of them. I chase them off because this one rose is all that is needed. I will not kill it for a bigger idea. Along come the horticulturalist experts to tell me how to make it even bigger and more beautiful. I chase them off because they don't appreciate the rose as it already is in all its splendor. I will not change this rose into another one. Along come the insecticide and herbicide specialists and gene-manipulators to tell me how to develop this rose into a stronger strain. I chase them off because they don't realize that letting it be is its best protection. It is strong enough if left alone. Along come the reporters and spin-doctors to make deals on how to publish its praise in a more professional, profitable and marketable way. I chase them off because the rose reports its own beauty.

It is the same with this community. I've seen, I've tried and I've done all kinds of programs and agendas and visions and strategies. They all without exception, I've concluded, do not appreciate what is. They all try to change it and add to it with the best of intentions and the best of efforts, but they do not realize that in the process they destroy it. I feel my primary job as a pastor is to just allow the rose to be the rose, to enjoy it, to praise it, and to let it be. Nothing more. Nothing less. This, in my opinion, is love. This, in my opinion, is what a pastor does: he or she loves the people and cares for them. Simple as that!

Invite to the Wedding of Truth and Passion (July 3, 2007)

Something dangerous comes with the turf I'm on. I have a passion for theological depth. I'm interested in the truth and that finds expression in my reading everything from biographies, brain science, philosophy, theology, atheism, people magazine… anything! On the other hand, I also have an intense interest in the summits of mystical insight, spiritual experience and passionate worship.

I think of the Baal Shem Tov, an intellectual Jewish mystic. Is it at all possible to search and embrace the depths of truth while at the same time scaling the heights of the spiritual life? It's rare to witness. I mostly see either one or the other. Those who pursue intellectuality and knowledge usually scorn spiritual experience, holding that only that which is rational is valid. Then there are those who pursue spiritual experience and disdain intellectual depth. I realize this is a generalization, but generally I think it's a fair assessment.

I think we need both. Like in the arts. I love art. So once in a while I like to listen to music that is thoughtful, insightful, prophetic and challenging. But sometimes I just like listening to music that soothes. Sometimes I like art that says something that needs to be said, no matter how harsh and offensive. But other times I like art that doesn't say anything except how spectacularly beautiful this world is. The height and the depth!

I pastor a church that has experienced some pretty interesting things. What I've found is that once you say you are interested in that whole charismatic realm, the magnetic pull towards big-church success, conferences, huge money, glamour, competition, visions, revelations, prophecies, international speakers and worship leaders, the gigantic money-cow of worship music, and all-around silliness is almost too much to resist. Let's all admit: the charismatic is a magnet for the crazy. But so is the intellect a magnet for a dead rationalism that just makes you want to scream for fresh air!

I believe rational truth and passionate experience make a beautiful marriage. But divorce is on the rise.

Freedom From Agendas (July 6, 2007)

Once in a while I'll get a blast of clarity. Usually when I'm driving. Like today when I was driving to the hospital to visit my friend. He hurt his back and is in a lot of pain. I was thinking how I do what many pastors do: study, pray, visit, counsel… simple things. But while I was thinking these thoughts I immediately felt myself arguing with something. I don't want to be burdened with an agenda. I don't want to burden our church community with an agenda. Not even lofty and noble ones. We are a society of friends, a community gathered together around Jesus. That's it. I encourage and nurture that. Simple as that! I don't spend time in my study figuring out how to save the world, how to grow the church, how to get more money out of people's pockets, how to promote this church's ministry, how

to enthrall our people more with sexy worship music, how to make myself more awesome before my people, how to get more people to hear about and come to our church. In fact, I reject the "how-to" disease altogether. Well, except maybe one: how to guard the church from all of that.

Again, I use the analogy of a relationship. Lisa and I don't have an agenda. We live fully every moment and the rest takes care of itself. You may try to convince me otherwise, but give up before you start. We have never once sat down and planned our future. We haven't even planned out the future of our children. Many of you might say, "Well, that's obviously your problem!" So be it! Just keep those nagging agendas away! We don't want anything to do with it. We truly believe we are healthier for it. I truly believe our church is healthier for it. It makes for better Christians, better people, and a more biblical existence. I know too many pastors, myself included, who have burned themselves out to keep up with a fantastic vision. My suspicions are getting stronger all the time: vision kills.

Learn Quick or Be Insane (July 11, 2007)

I am really not trying to be difficult. I'm not trying to just be a stick-in-the-mud, a naysayer, a pain in the butt. But I've seen something, tasted something, heard something, felt something, smelled something, experienced something. And I'm not willing to pretend it didn't happen. It resounds with truth for me. You see, I've gone through extremely painful experiences, not only in the church, but at the hands of the church. I'm not looking for pity. I abhor pity. Just as I abhor the opposite side of the same coin: flattery. The things that I've experienced have taught me something. They've taught me something very, very important. I've come to see the primacy of freedom for the human being. And I've also seen how dreams, visions, agendas, goals, desires and passions enslave people. I've been there myself!

When I went through the horrific church split 10 years ago, it tore my heart out. The church was the fulfillment of a dream of mine. When it crashed, someone advised me to simply get another dream. I immediately saw the vacuous but tempting trap that was being set for me. I rejected it. Since then, I reject dreams. I deny visions. However, a few times the temptations were too great and I fell to the temptation, only for my suspicions to be quickly and violently confirmed: visions and dreams by default destroy the beauty of the present and what is. I try not to concern myself with tomorrow. I endeavor to live in the now. I love what there is for me to love. I live my days. And I encourage others to do the same, including our church community.

Does this mean nothing gets done? Certainly not! I believe that this act of being present, living now, focusing on what is, centering down into the actual, is an enormous source of energy. Hasn't it been said that doing the same mistake over and over again but expecting different results is the definition of insanity? But we in the church do exactly this! I'm done with it! We're to be fools, I'm told. Sure, but not insane.

Explaining the Inexplicable (July 13, 2007)

I've suspected for quite a long time: my style of ministry isn't conducive to church growth or success. At least that's been my experience. Even though I feel a deep conviction that I am to pastor the way I do, it hasn't amounted to much. My church hasn't grown. It has no more money. We don't have any amazing stories to tell. At least nothing that would make headlines in all the major Christian testimonials. In fact, my style has caused my church to split, caused me to be dismissed from another ministry, and seen people come only to eventually go over the years. There is a solid group of people here who understand this and support it. Plus, evidently from my blog, there are some of you out there who get it. I don't know what I can do about it without compromising what I know to be true.

Not many people understand me. Not many people understand my style of ministry. I can't explain it, although I try. That's what this blog is for... to explain the inexplicable to you, my confused reader. I don't lead. I don't have a vision. My teaching is offensive and disappointing. I get that all the time. I've gotten that for years.

There's so much muscle-flexing in the church today. I do this! I do that! Look how accomplished I am! Look how big I am! Look how wealthy I've become! Look how influential I am! Look how I'm changing the world! Look how effective I am! But I'm unwilling to flex muscle except when it comes to the protection of my flock, my people. And what I feel we most need protection from is the hard muscle of the present-day church. Not the world! I choose to be weak as a shepherd. Our people, for the most part I believe, choose to be weak as a church. I reject muscular attainments that we religious people aspire to and the church craves. I wait for a better life. New life. Genuine, authentic and true life! I thirst for living water, not pumped and processed water. I can't explain it, but I'll keep trying. This is the cross to me. Thanks for your patience.

Are You A Great Resource? (July 17, 2007)

Excuse me while I continue to attempt to articulate what I mean. Something else I've been thinking of is that I need to resist the temptation to see my people or my church as a *resource*. This is not to mean that it isn't a resource. In fact, I think my church community is a powerful collection of unusually gifted, passionate, authentic, wise, unique individuals who can change worlds. The temptation is to see this community as a means to an end. Rather than see them as people, I see them as a way to influence their surroundings or change the world or do what I think they should do.

Almost all the stuff I read to do with church falls in this category of seeing the church as a resource, and even seeing individuals as resources. It is as if I saw my wife Lisa as a "wife" or a "sex-partner" or "co-parent". It isn't that she isn't all these things, but I can't look at her as those things. She is first and foremost Lisa, a person who voluntarily loves me and receives my love. And out of that reality spins the lesser realities of roles, activities and projects. I must believe that reveling in that love makes manifest the resource aspect of the love relationship. It is out of love that sex, partnership and home-life emerges.

It's the same with the church. It is out of personal spiritual health as well as communal spiritual health that all the resources naturally emerge. And the emergence of these resources should be as delightfully spontaneous as sex is at its best or as joyfully surprising as the appearance of fruit on the vine is to the gardener. And for me, spiritual health means loving others and being loved freely and in freedom.

When people look at me and see a man with a variety of gifts, talents, abilities, interests and hobbies (let's say), I reject it immediately when they look at me as a resource, as a potential, as a pool for something greater, as a means to some end. This is a false and destructive way to look at me as a person. I reject this maltreatment vehemently. It's the same for my church community. When people look at it as a source for something else, as a pool for some greater idea or vision, as a bank of influence to change something, I run them off like wolves because they are hungry for the taste and satisfaction that my beautiful people would supply them.

No Vision No Policy (July 25, 2007)

Years ago I read David Herbert Donald's, *Lincoln*, and found it profoundly applicable to my own life and situation as a pastor. Lincoln himself knew what it meant to be accused of not having a vision, of having no moral standard and of being a poor leader. I don't think Lincoln had a vision except for the freedom of all people. But I don't think that is necessarily a vision as in a corporate goal to achieve. Rather, it is something to be proclaimed and practiced. The freedom of all people is a reality only cloaked in the evil of humanity and this world. The emancipation of ourselves and others is an urgent and instantaneous necessity that must be manifested at every instance. No vision is required. There's also no seeing ahead but to the next immediate point. Here's one of the quotes from Donald that impacted me most:

"From Lincoln's fatalism derived some of his most lovable traits: his compassion, his tolerance, his willingness to overlook mistakes. That belief did not, of course, lend him to lethargy or dissipation. Like thousands of Calvinists who believed in

predestination, he worked indefatigably for a better world...for himself, for his family, and for his nation. But it helped to buffer the many reverses that he experienced and enabled him to continue a strenuous life of aspiration."

"It also made for a pragmatic approach to problems, a recognition that if one solution as fated not to work another could be tried. 'My policy is to have no policy' became a kind of motto from Lincoln... a motto that infuriated the sober, doctrinaire people around him who were inclined to think that the President had no principals either. He might have offended his critics less if he had more often used the analogy he gave James G. Blaine when explaining his course on Reconstruction: 'The pilots on our Western rivers steer from point to point as they call it "setting the course" of the boat no further than they can see; and that is all I propose to myself in this great problem.'"

Both statements suggest Lincoln's reluctance to take the initiative and make bold plans; he preferred to respond to the actions of others. They also show why Lincoln in his own distinctively American way had the quality John Keats defined as forming ' a Man of Achievement', that quality

> 'which Shakespeare possessed so enormously: Negative Capability, that is when a man is capable of being in uncertainties, Mysteries, doubts, without any irritable reaching after fact and reason.'

How To Get Free (July 26, 2007)

You can read Amaris' comment from yesterday's post "My Policy is to Have No Policy" to see what motivated me to write today's post. Here's what she asked me:

"There is a block when we try to move into freedom and I think that some of these reasons are why. So my last question is, what are some practical things we can do to help ourselves and others move into freedom? We are going to feel the slap of the fresh air, we can't escape that, so now where do we go?" This is my quick answer:

1. First of all I think we need to have an honest **appraisal** of ourselves. We need to observe honestly all that is going on in our brains. I think we need to realize how enslaved we are. I know so many people enslaved by a vision of what they think they should be or what others think they should be. I was just talking with a young woman this morning who doesn't feel free to make her own life-

decision out of fear of disappointing her parents' dream for her. We need to recognize, in our own minds, the things that we are enslaved by… even the very noble and acceptable things. That is the first step.

2. The next step is **automatic**. I believe that when we recognize our enslavements, we are immediately before an open door and within an opened room. About 11 years ago I was feeling completely trapped and hopeless in a church situation. I had a dream one night and woke up the next day a free man. Nothing had changed except my thinking. My mind had changed, and I was free. Life's never been the same since. When we recognize and name our captors in our own minds, they immediately turn into vapor.

3. The next step is to **practice** your liberty. Act free! Expect opposition. Expect to disappoint people. Expect to get shot at. A truly liberated person is often quite offensive. But those who hunger and thirst for freedom are inspired by such people. Live free and speak free and others will take their cue from you. You can't make people be free, but only describe what this freedom is and live it. Take marriage for example. Lisa and I have been married for over 27 years. I prefer young lovers to watch us live and love each other rather than sit down and be counseled and taught by us. Same with freedom! If you think, live, and speak as a free person, others around you will explore the possibility for themselves.

I'm sorry if this is way too simplistic. But I honestly believe it is as simple as that. This isn't to say it isn't hard. It requires much courage and energy to examine ourselves. That is the hardest part. If you succeed here, the rest is gravy.

Narrow is the Gate (August 8, 2007)

Here is something I wrote in my journal Sunday afternoon,

August 5, verbatim. It explains some of the paradoxical anguish I experience trying to write on nakedpastor:

> My problem is I can't seem to articulate clearly what I sense. It is something very, very simple. And not even that. It is thin, narrow, slender like a thread. It isn't a vision or a goal because it just is. It is what is, so how can it be a vision or a goal because it already is!? It is so simple that it offends the mind. When you walk it, it is so razor's edge that is causes your heart to fear, wonder, doubt. It wants to turn back. The danger is the words I use to describe it actually can pollute what I'm trying to describe. I feel like I'm trying to weed the garden of all that is useless to express this tender shoot, and my words are like more weeds because they are inadequate and crowding. But when you find this place, or when you discover that you are already in this place, devoid of all that is peripheral, it is full of love and benediction.

This is my attempt to explain my attempt to explain what is truly religious, what is truly community, what is truly God. The more I rationalize, the more I write, the more I speak, the more cluttered this place becomes. Like friends of mine and I talked about this morning this morning: all this debate and argument is useless. It is nothing but noise that transforms no one. Before him let all the earth keep silence. I think the more words there are, the more it indicates that we aren't before that which we call God.

Starting From Scratch (August 21, 2007)

I talk with lots of pastors and I talk with lots of church-goers and non-church-goers. Here's what I'm discovering that's pretty consistent with all groups: pastors are burning out and full of frustration and resentment because they don't feel free to be themselves or to be authentic. Church-goers and non-... same thing: we are not allowed to be ourselves or be authentic. For the vast majority of those connected with church in any way, it is one of the most inhumane and soul-murderous thing in their lives. So, I have an idea. Why don't we all decide right now, starting now, that we all just be ourselves? Why don't we let down our pretenses and allow others to do the same? Why don't we just start being authentically who we are and respect others as they try to do the same? Why don't we all stop playing Church and playing Christian and just be the people that we are? If I am me and you are you and we are the church, then let's relax and let that reality exist without impinging our expectations and desires and goals and visions upon this reality! We get so anal about needing to live up to some idea we have of what a Christian is and we get so obsessive about what we think the church should look and act like that we miss the fact that we already are these things.

I realize as I write this that some of you will feel compelled to write, "*You are right, nakedpastor! We should only be in the image of Christ, and remember that the church is his body!*" There are so many problems with this that I can't even begin to comment on it. First of all, I say discover who you are! And look and see what the church already is with clear and unambitious eyes. Look at yourself and others with love. Let down your guard, your expectations, your religious ideas and finally notice what already is! Scratch all the superfluous. Then you might be able to know the naked self it is you are surrendering to this that you call the Christ.

Beauty Not Always in Eye of Beholder (September 14, 2007)

Beauty. Recognize and appreciate the beauty. Respect it. I had a few people mention the fine-art photograph I had on my post yesterday, Living Without a Goal. This piece of art is beautiful. The comments people gave are thoughtful and beautiful in their own right. But it goes further than flesh and form. When someone comes into our community, do we see

them as they are, sure… with all their struggles and weaknesses… but what about their own beauty. Each one is beautiful. Is each one seen? Is each one respected?

When beauty is recognized and appreciated, then our urges to change it become redundant. With the photo yesterday, if you really see it and appreciate it, how would you want to change her, or change Howard's photograph? When you see a beautiful flower, how would you want to manipulate it into anything else other than what it already is? I am surrounded by people who have been under pressure to change. I have been under pressure to change, to conform to someone else's expectations, to their vision they have of me. What that does is tell the person that in fact they aren't beautiful at all but ugly. Appreciate and respect the beauty in other people. But first you have to see it. So we try to create an environment where people can freely blossom in the good soil of love and respect.

Your House is Burning Down (September 28, 2007)

I really don't know what to say. I appreciate your comments, but we are still not seeing it. I'm still in a season of speechlessness. I'm at a place where I feel like my whole continent is shaking at the roots. The whole world is crashing in. The paradigm I have been comfortably operating in is imploding, and I can't presently see where else to go. I am a man in a house that is fully ablaze. There is no time to decide anything. It is only time to run. Run away from the flame. Get out of the house. NOW!

I don't think it is helpful to simply tweak the system. I don't think it is important anymore to upgrade our theology. I don't think it does a bit of good to provide a new edition to our doctrine. I think it is a waste of time to solidify a new position. Not another dogmatic theology! Not another denomination! Not another congregation with a new vision! Not another religious blog! Not another spirituality! Not another strategy! Not another program! I'm sick of these. They are lukewarm. I spew them out of my mouth! They are tasteless, unhealthy, lack any nutrition, and are in fact toxic.

I want to make it clear that I am not unhappy with the community I am a part of. I have no problem with the communities of people out there. It is something else. It is the boat we sail in. It is the overarching paradigm that constantly tries to confine us by conforming us to itself. I think our community is quite free in many ways, and I appreciate it. It has been grueling but rewarding because of that. But we are still under the yoke of bondage because we all come to the community with visions of what it should be rather than seeing what it actually is. We are still not entirely free of expectations and the resulting judgments. Which means we still have not come to a place of love. We have yet to die to all that came before. The cross is still before us, and we are not yet nailed to it.

Friends at the End of the Day (October 24, 2007)

A friend sent me a small note that said, among other things, *"Enjoy the companionship of those who call on the Lord with pure hearts"* (2 Timothy 2:22). It meant a lot to me, especially today, and I'll tell you why.

People have left our community. Again. And I think more will leave. It's hard to take. I don't resent them. I'm not angry. People are free to choose what they want. I don't imagine I have everything everybody needs. But when new people come (and I hope new ones will) I always feel a little insecure. People are often drawn to the strong sense of community and the potential for friendship. Our music is passionate. People pray. The teaching, shared by many, is good and solid. Plus we have great parties. But I always wonder how long it's going to take new people to realize that there is nothing else. What you see is what you get. Period!

I remember quite a while ago someone complaining to me about our community and about the way I do leadership. Well, mainly the fact that I don't do leadership. I'm not a strong leader. The people of the community are great. There is authenticity. Worship's great. Teaching's great. But let's get a vision! We need a purpose! Let's organize and DO something! I asked this woman why it wasn't enough that we had worship, fellowship, teaching, prayer, and that people were helping others. She was drawn by all these things. She loved the authenticity, how real people were, how honest and sincere, how radical and rebellious against the machine they

©nakedpastor

were. But she wanted more. She wanted the slick glamour that other churches have with all their programs and outreaches and ministries and appearance of health. I said that I didn't think that you could have both. It's one or the other. If you want genuine and authentic community, I think you have to neglect the pursuit of success. If you want success, you have to neglect authenticity. It's form or substance. Choose one. She chose. She left.

It is happening again and will happen again. I shared this with a friend this morning and he said that he had been praying for me and felt that there was a cross in my future. Lovely! But he also said that he prayed that God would give me companions for the journey. Sometimes I wonder if it might come down to just me and a few friends at the end of the day. I hope not. I hope there will be a crowd. But I won't bet on it.

A Fork in the Road (November 2, 2007)

After the innocent little cartoon that I posted the other day here, I received a few remarks disagreeing with it. I know I have discussed this over and over again. Here I go again.

The other night I met with some people who question why I don't have a mission statement or a vision statement or a set of goals for the church. The premise is: once we know who we want to be, then we can work towards being that. If you aim at nothing, that's what you're going to hit! I know this is the most popular and widely assumed and accepted wisdom, but I reject it completely. For a few reasons:

1. In my own life, I've discovered that setting a vision for myself of who I want to be reveals a deep repugnance of who I am and coats it with ideals. It is an ancient remedy for denying and escaping from suffering and is a denial of reality.
2. As a part of the church for years, I have seen how over and over again the vision, mission or goals of a community stifle the life of individuals and violently molds the community into the shape someone or some others have for it.
3. As a pastor, I have come to the conclusion that people and communities are healthier and even prosper when

some ideal of who or what they should be is not applied to them.

I told my friends the other night that we come to a fork in the road: the one to the left is where we make ourselves or others conform to a vision. This may lead to the appearance of success, but I think it is often superficial and very often the culture of violence. The one to the right is where there is no vision or ideal imposed upon ourselves or others. In my experience this leads to extraordinary freedom and authenticity. In my experience, this leads to incredible fruitfulness. Some friends say to me, *"Well, then THAT'S your vision!"* No, as lofty and beautiful and tempting as this sounds, it is not, because even to apply this vision to people locks them in, and to be locked in to anything is bondage and slavery of some sort.

Again, I emphasize, this is in my experience and observation. You may disagree. Of course, you are free to.

Judging and Despising (November 23, 2007)

Tucked away in Romans 14:10 is an obscure little verse that I feel is absolutely crucial to the understanding of community health. I remember in my younger years arguing vehemently for this or that side of the argument: whether a believer could drink or not, etc… or whether he or she shouldn't if in the company of those who had problems with drinking. Oh yes, how well I remember those debates! Then I remember in more recent years arguing for the sake of freedom and railing against those who would oppress it. But gradually the importance of this verse has changed this and captivated my mind:

"Why do you pass judgment on your brother or sister? Or you, why do you despise your brother or sister?"

And this is what it all comes down to: *judging* and *despising*. I see these two things operating all the time in our community. On the one hand you have someone who has worked hard at becoming an exemplary believer, who practices his or her idea of religion, abstains from certain foods, liquids and practices, and observes spiritual disciplines that would put us to shame, and what happens: they judge those who do not observe the same rules or follow their spiritual walk. They look at them religiously with holy judgment because they are smudgy in their unsaintliness and impure in their spiritual walk. They judge them as sinners, or at least less holy.

Then, on the other hand, someone thinks they've come to some revelation, directly from God of course, and has reached a certain level of maturity, spiritual insight, practice and liberty, and what happens? They despise those who haven't reached the level they're at, who haven't had the same revelation, who aren't as spiritually insightful, who aren't as liberated. They despise them as spiritually undeveloped children. In both cases, the judgers and despisers look down on others. They don't love or respect them.

Ah, it never ends. These two things happen simultaneously and perpetually in the life of the community. When we think it is theological exactitude or moral perfection or missional vision that is the point, these are not the point at' all. They are important. But they are only the extras. In the last analysis, it's not going to be what theology you embraced, what spiritual disciplines you practiced, what vision you crafted and pursued, but did you love one another. I'm beginning to wonder if we'll ever, ever get that.

A Boy's Disappointment (January 3, 2008)

The reason those of us who keep looking for miracles, signs and wonders are called adulterous is because we want a god other than the one we already have.

I had a bit of a revelation over the holidays. I saw myself as a little boy. My mind is filled with dreams and expectations and desires. They continuously get disappointed. So, as a result, my life is filled with disappointment. I don't see these expectations fulfilled. I am sad far too often. I've been advised over and over again that I need to recast my visions, to adjust my dreams, to work harder to see my expectations come to pass. I've tried that and it is fruitless. Buddha realized that too. I've come to the conclusion that dreams and visions and the pursuit of signs and wonders is not only unhealthy, but, as Jesus said, adulterous. And I am one of those adulterous people completely surrounded by adulterous people.

This last year I saw many reasonable expectations meet with wild disappointment. I agree with Paul who agreed with the Old Testament, that we are all sinners and that all our feet are swift to shed blood. I no longer put my hope in people. I no longer put my hope in their strategies. They are dead-ends. I choose to put my hope in God, whatever that means. I'm going to be content with the god I got. Or, rather, who got me. I somehow know that if one woman or one man was transformed by the renewing of his or her mind… well… look out world!

Putin, the Church & Dissent (January 18, 2008)

I recently read *Time Magazine's Person of the Year* issue for 2007… the articles on Vladimir Putin, the President of Russia. The more I read the more parallels popped out at me between what Putin is doing in or for Russia and the modern-day church. Here's the tension: Putin is getting Russia back on the map as a world-player. Wealth is increasing, poverty decreasing, their national debt of 2 billion has been paid off, and on and on. It is almost all because of Putin's strength, vision and steely determination as a leader. On the other hand, there have been costs to this success: Putin has shut down TV stations and newspapers, jailed businessmen who challenged the Kremlin, neutralized opposition parties and arrested anyone who resisted his rule. In spite of this, Putin's popularity ratings hover over 70%. The conclusion is that Russians would rather have security and success than liberty. I think as a gloss veneer to the questionable reality, it is called a *"sovereign democracy"*.

As one author, who was persecuted for his writings, put it: *"Russians come to love their bonds"*.

I by no means wish to insist that this is an easy tension to decipher or solve. In fact, the trend is irresistible. If I were in Russia, which would I prefer? Poverty or liberty? The fact is, Putin's method of rule seems to be working for Russia's success on the world stage. But the price seems high to me. Journalists end up missing or murdered. Putin's regime suggests that this is being done by people wishing to put Putin in a bad light. Few people would insist that Putin himself would be corrupt. Why, he's a Christian and reads the Bible! Bush read his soul by looking in his eyes and saw a man of conviction. But the power that he exerts and the regime that surrounds him has created, some believe, this culture of unquestionable autocratic rule. Putin is indeed creating a strong state, and anyone who stands in the way of it (it is implicitly but definitely understood) will pay for it. Some of the dissenting Russian journalists interviewed requested to remain nameless for fear of repercussions. They knew they would lose their jobs, or worse! There is no outright blanket of terror, but it is underwritten throughout the culture that dissent will be isolated and punished.

I am a dissenter. I realize that. But it is because I love the church. Not because I wish to see her destroyed. Who would question the courageous loyalty of a Russian journalist wishing to uncover the questionable policies and practices of their beloved country? This same tension exists in the church as anywhere: we've come to love our bonds because we are granted a measure of success by keeping them. The church, I think, is willing to sacrifice basic human and civil liberties for good and noble results. We prefer success or even just stability to freedom of expression. Freedom of expression is messy and unmanageable.

So after I read that issue of time, I set it back down on our coffee table more determined to raise my voice of dissent, to persist in voicing my opinion, and, bottom line, to believe in the Holy Catholic church and the communion of saints at all costs. I will not be enamored by success or relevance in the world if it costs the life or liberty of even just one.

In Love and In Death (January 24, 2008)

Is it possible to care for someone without having designs for him or her? Is it possible to love someone without having an agenda, no matter how glorious or noble? Is it possible to respect someone without having dreams or wishes for that person? These are very real questions that I ask. They are not hypothetical either, but real and urgent and necessary.

Jesus got angry with the teachers because they were laying burdens upon the people, burdens no doubt birthed from the teachers' well-informed and studied dreams, desires, wishes, agendas and plans for the people. I don't think for a second that their intentions were evil, but good and admirable. Could they love and teach the people without burdening them at all? Could they teach them without their teaching being pregnant with expectations? Could they love them with their desires as a community completely detached?

This is the problem: not that we need to purify our wishes for others, but to crucify them; not that we must make lovelier strings to attach to our love, but to cut them off altogether; not that we must baptize our agendas, but to lay them down once and for all; not that we must passionately make our visions more heavenly, but to forsake them now. What destroys true community is the layers of expectation, agenda, vision and wishes that are pressed upon it. This is why love is very much like death... because in both we must learn to let go. And this is why, my friends, we refuse to love... because it is too much like death... death to ourselves and all our desires.

What Holds Us Together (February 15, 2008)

I've been thinking about what holds us together as a community. This has been on my mind because of the many people I hear from, almost daily, who are hungering for true community but can't find it. I see this especially in the young, who have no interest in what used to define community. They are looking for something else.

It has become obvious to me that, for instance, it isn't the marriage license, the certificate, the paper that holds a marriage together. It has also become increasingly obvious to me that neither do the vows, the promises, or the wedding ceremony, hold a marriage together. I've also become aware that compatibility, having things in common, sharing a common goal or vision, is not the cohesive glue in a relationship either.

Translate this analogy of marriage into community life and you have the same thing. Being a member does not hold a community together. Being a part of a church doesn't keep it. Neither do the sacraments or vows or promises. Neither does theological unity or common goals or a shared vision hold it together.

It can only be love, mutual love that holds a relationship or a community together. What I am trying to say is that we have to get to the place where we realize that we just can't expect people to remain committed to each other because it is expected, or promises were made, or there is uniformity in whatever area, or that there is a common goal we've set for them. People, especially younger people, aren't interested in uniformity, conformity, or forms of any kind. There must be genuine acceptance, honesty, authenticity, freedom, and love for community to work. This requires intense energy from each person, and nothing outside of themselves can be called upon to ensure the relationship will work… no authority, document, ruler, goal, vision, practice, or tradition.

This is why I don't strive for theological uniformity, homogeneity in life-style, protocol, authority, submission, legal agreement, or anything of the sort. These no longer matter. It comes down to love, its practice. That is, the way of love.

Shortcuts to Maturity (May 2, 2008)

There are no shortcuts to maturity. Someone has an intense spiritual experience, insight, or revelation, and the impression is that this person suddenly will be more mature, responsible and exemplary. This is often not the case. How many men and women have we seen who set themselves up or are set up by others as spiritually advanced or insightful only to find, in due time, that they are just as human and fallible as the rest of us?

Take Ken Wilber's article on "*The Strange Case of Adi Da*", the Fiji guru who initially had Wilber's support, only for it to be withdrawn later because of the intense controversy surrounding the "pathological" guru. Wilber writes:

> *Over the years I have made numerous very strong and sometimes contradictory statements about Adi Da, mostly because he is a very strong and sometimes contradictory personality. . . . I called attention to the fact that, even though Da might be highly spiritually realized, he seemed to have several problematic, perhaps even pathological, aspects to his personality and the way he was running his community. . . . Contradictory? Perhaps, but only because Da is contradictory. Contradictory and problematic... deeply problematic.*

This applies to the Christian and church realm too. We see our youth go off to camp or missions or whatever and come back incredibly zealous and inspirational. We love this and encourage it, but we must not put the burden of expectation upon them that they are more mature, responsible or exemplary than they actually are. It is the same with tele-evangelists. It is also the same with the more visible and commendable members of our communities of faith. We must not allow their zeal, intelligence, influence, or vision to blind us to their frail humanity, their solidarity with the rest of the fallen human race. It is not fair to them to elevate them above the mundane work of personal development because of their extraordinary giftedness.

This does not mean we suppress the gifting of individuals. No matter how immature or mature anyone is, their contribution to the community and to the world is encouraged, nurtured, supported and valued. But not at the expense of their own personal growth, transformation and stability. It is possible, and indeed probable, that one can be *"highly spiritually realized"*, and yet have deep pathological issues that must be struggled with and healed, I think preferably in the context of a safe and healthy community.

Anti-Strategy (May 8, 2008)

I take no credit or praise for my community. Any credit or praise belongs to the community itself. I have built nothing. I have constructed nothing. I have succeeded in doing nothing.

I have grown nothing. In fact, I make it my purpose to not build anything with these people. What I have around me is a community of people who willingly and voluntarily desire to be in relationship with each other and to gather together. Ephesians 4: 3 says to "*keep the unity of the Spirit*". Unity, or community, is not something we have to build, but keep. I therefore see my primary task as preventing obstacles and barriers from interfering in this reality. I'm a weeder. When I think of it, my activity as a pastor is negative, as non-activity. It is to prevent interference, remove obstacles, clear impediments and reject deterrents to unity and community. It is so popular now to have the excessive baggage of plans, visions, goals, renewal, and programmed growth, that true authenticity and true community is difficult if not impossible. What I try to nurture is an environment free of restrictions to the unity that is already ours. This means free people gathering freely in the reality of freedom. Why complicate it?

I am confident that as the weeds are kept at bay, fruit will grow in individuals and in the community. But this is not my doing. We could go further with the analogy to say that good teaching and life experience is fertilizer, but I wanted to try to communicate what my strategy is for pastoring a healthy community. It is anti-strategy. It is to *not* include, assimilate or integrate strategies to create, erect, build or grow something. It is free, I hope, of my ambitions, goals, visions or desires for these people and this community. My only desire is for them to be free, and free to experience the unity that is theirs. And in that freedom is their possibility for a fruitful life. This is not radical. It is anti-radical. Perhaps you can see this? It is difficult to articulate.

Commonalities (May 14, 2008)

Let me think out loud for a minute. When people gather together in community around a *commonality**, the potential for it to be overtaken by the principalities and powers is immediate. This is what we must constantly wrestle against. There is the temptation for my community identified as Rothesay Vineyard identifying with the principality called "Rothesay Vineyard", which is the composite of all human and angelic desires, wishes, agendas and expectations for Rothesay Vineyard. There is the even broader danger of us identifying with the principalities called "Vineyard", "Church" and "Christian". It is most difficult for a community to simply be a gathering of people without the pressure of ideals being pressed upon it. I consider it injurious to our community to imagine what this community should be. I regard it toxic to communal life to impose upon it my plans or goals. Vision corrupts the community that is. To even talk in passionately imaginative ways about what our community could be feels adulterous to me. It perverts love into fantasy. The principalities and powers, like in every other age, are presently in full swing. These things need to be discerned. Why? Because they appear brilliant and good to the contemporary mind! But they have one purpose, and that is first to oppress, then to possess, then to ultimately deliver death to the person and to the people.

*I realize this isn't a word, but I invented it to describe something around which a community agrees, whether it be marriage, family, religion, belief, faith, politic, capitalism, etc., etc…

Flee to the Desert (May 20, 2008)

Every once in a while I come to the realization that I don't believe in church as it is. I don't wish to support it. I don't want to perpetuate its existence. I don't want to reinforce its rules, its politics, its agendas, its programs. I want to get out of it altogether. I yearn to remove myself from this game completely and forever. I want, like the earliest hermits such as St. Anthony in Egypt, to retreat to the remotest desert and weave baskets. And I would do this not only as a way to get back in touch with raw simplicity and truth, but also as a demonstration of protest against the ecclesiastical system and its managers. Within, I'm done with it. When, oh when, will we ever realize that all we are doing with all of our ideas, visions, agendas, revolutions and reforms is tweaking that which imprisons us? We are the captains of modification. The result: people come along, take one look at the dolled-up corpse of our refined church, and say, "My, it looks really good!" just before we close the casket!

I don't know how to do this. I don't know how we, as friends of faith, can gather together without the complications of structure, institution, government, mores, politics, laws, hierarchy, expectations, agendas and goals interfering with community. I don't know how we can stop church from obstructing fellowship. I don't know how we can stop religion from murdering humanity. It's almost like our marriage is getting in the way of our love. Can it be done? I have to believe it can and must be done. Otherwise, the demons have won.

I had a dream the other night. There was a riverbed and a river flowing through it. This riverbed was Jesus. So the river was somehow Jesus too. This river was somehow within me, like within my chest. Suddenly, the river began to become engorged until it overflowed its banks. Then this river covered the whole earth. I awoke in a cloud of peace and joy. But I also awoke deeply troubled because this has practical implications for my life that I haven't even begun to unpack yet.

Leeks and Liberty (May 21, 2008)

It is obvious all that religion has done nothing to improve the human condition. In fact, it continues to perpetuate division, violence and death. Although it may appear to be development, it is only the evolution of ideas and their systems that occurs. Evolution has happened and will continue to happen. This is in some ways good as our sciences, organizations, technologies, politics, etc., evolve. But inevitably we will continue to use these developments not only for progress, but for destruction.

I just had lunch with a friend who suggested that indeed there is evolution in the way we do church. I agree. He is going to a church that would be considered quite radical and advanced in terms of how to do it. However, it has become painfully plain to me that evolution is not what is best. But we give up the best for the good, as always. All the strategies out there for improving church are just gimmicks. They are participating in the evolutionary process. Some are more radical, racing towards new innovations and renovations. Some just go with the flow, roughly reflecting the surrounding culture's revisions. Others are counter-revolutionary, not only putting on the brakes, but dropping into reverse to restore traditional thought and practice. But all these are destined to perish because they are nothing but variations on the evolutionary process. And this will get us only back to where we started.

Transformation into a new creation: that is the best. But we are in too much of a hurry to stop and consider what this means. We are required right now to perform. We cater continuously to taste. There is no time to pay attention to this problem. I love the people of my community. I do not wish to abandon them. I think we are on to something. But we are still not expressing the freedom that is ours. We are still slaves to the evolutionary process. I think in many ways we are afraid of what transformation might mean. I think we are afraid of what a

new creation might look like and what it might require. Leeks and onions might not be the best thing on the menu, but at least it's a guaranteed meal. So we linger longingly in the land of our slavery.

Actually, when I think about it, it is probably me who is afraid.

Reform or Freedom? (May 28, 2008)

Is it possible for people to gather in complete freedom? I

continue to put this question because it is vital to the freedom of the individual and to the community. I am passionate about exploring this issue. I also think it is crucial that the question remains open because as soon as someone thinks he has the answer the results will be catalogued, published, then legislated.

People get upset over such cartoons as I published earlier today. Some are upset because they are convinced that the church as it is does need reform… that it must either change or die. Others are upset because they detect an undertone of disdain for the church. I have come to the conclusion that church reform is useless. I appreciate the Protestant principle, the Reformed tradition, its theologians and ideas. But the proposal that the church is reformed and always reforming reflects the endless cycle we are trapped within. It betrays the fallen condition we are not necessarily consigned to as free men and women or as communities. This will not nourish or protect our personal or corporate freedom.

Is there a way we can become entirely free as individuals? Perhaps it isn't even a "way", but a reality that is ours that we must instantly realize and enjoy. Then, can free people gather in such a way as to respect one another's freedom and not impair it, but to give it the opportunity for fullest expression in the context of community? Of course, this implies love, which necessarily implies mutual surrender, sacrifice and service. But can it be done? Can we gather free of designs, visions, plans, goals, purposes, expectations and conformations? Can we gather in love with love itself as the means and the end?

I have not yet seen it on a consistent basis. I have seen glimpses of it. They are beautiful moments beyond words. These are just momentary states, not a permanent stage yet.

I'm Repeating Myself! I'm Repeating Myself! (June 16, 2008)

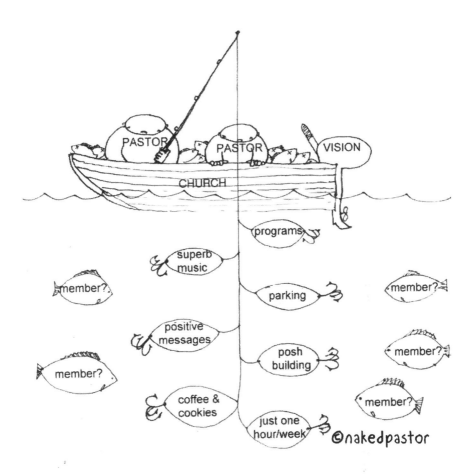

One of my more faithful commentators made this comment on my post last week called Designer Theology:

> *"Nakedpastor: do you find that you have to have the same arguments over and over again with yourself? Or are there things you take as a given? It seems to be you could realign your foundation over and over again and never really get as far as installing windows."*

I realize I seem to be repeating myself. But it's only because what is true is very simple and only so much can be said in a variety of ways. We live in a world swimming with principles, secrets, methods, truths, strategies, and more. It is a veritable ocean of ideas. I, in a sense, reject all this. I thoroughly refuse to believe that anyone can come up with a better idea or method or strategy to revolutionize, change or renew the church. I reject it all. Simple as that! So, all the ideas, methods or revolutions… I question at a most fundamental level. Axe to the roots! Shake the foundations!

Again, I'll compare our community to my family. I don't want anyone coming along with how to make my family better. I don't want strategies to use on my family to improve things. I don't want steps to increase the quality of our relationships. We are a family, so in a very real sense I'm not trying to build it. It is built. It is there. Love it. I am a part of a community. It is already a church. It is there. Love it. That's all there is. I'm not trying to build it. Now… as soon as I say that I know that people will quote me scriptures about building the church. But those passages aren't talking about church growth, strategies to improve it, programs to support, promote or advertise it, or visions to expand it. I think it is talking about truth. I think it is talking about, in biblical terms, the gospel. I think a person and a community grows through the acknowledgement, acquisition, appropriation and application of truth. Numbers aren't the concern primarily.

So, yes, on the one hand I keep repeating myself. On the other hand, what else can I say in a world exploding with a new idea and strategy for me to consider and adopt every day of the week? I realize too that some say that my anti-strategy is actually a strategy. Call it what you will, but I don't think so because there is no movement in it. It is a place of rest I have great difficulty describing. But I will keep doing so, no matter how many words it takes or how often it is misunderstood. Why? Because I believe it is a place of rest and peace that all people have a right to, including people in religious communities.

Symptomatography (June 23, 2008)

I would like to use a word that I can't find in any of my dictionaries: "symptomatography". I would like to use it because I believe that all the issues and problems that we normally treat are symptoms of a deeper malignant disease. It is crucial that we recognize this and develop the skill of

Now THIS is my kind of church!

diagnosing the disease and the symptoms it presents. The reason being that we settle with simply treating the symptom with band-aids... an interim measure that may decrease or even provisionally eliminate the presentation of the disease. Anyone can apply disinfectant, salve, gauze, band-aids; and some can even cut and sew. But fewer people can actually diagnose and confront the disease.

I recognized this early in my relationship with Lisa. It was through our commitment to prove our love over the long haul that I learned that everything I do that hurts Lisa is not just a simple mistake or oversight. I began to realize that all my little trespasses against her were symptoms of deeper issues that needed astute diagnosis and serious attention if I wanted to stop hurting her. This is why, in the church context, I try to take the time to diagnose every little problem that comes along. This is why all the terrible things I have experienced in the name of love, God and the church are not simply written off as little slips or slights in human error, but significant manifestations of a deeper malevolence that need brutally honest detection and committed treatment. The abuse I've suffered at the hands of church leaders, other Christians, the insane chaos of a church split, being fired from another international ministry for "insubordination", etc., are all not just little episodic blemishes in church life, but revelatory symptoms of deeply serious defects, profound flaws, and continental faults that need immediate and radical treatment.

I am not willing to say: *"Well, let's go back and try that again!"* Why? Why go back and apply the same old remedies to the same old problems *ad nauseam*? I contend that we need to cut open the chest, stretch apart the ribs and go in… straight for the heart! Or shave the head, peel back the face, saw open the skull and hold the diseased brain in our very hands!

My Supplemental Jesus (June 26, 2008)

I want to consider our supplemental Jesus. Most of our writing and talking is supplemental in nature. We get so excited with and carried away by the next new idea, the next new leader, the next new book, the next new method. But there is really nothing truly new about it all. They are accruals upon the past. They are installments on a faulty loan. They are renovations on a condemned building. It is our attempt to stretch an already stretched old wineskin. We customize what we already have. Like an old car that has been condemned to the scrap heap… it doesn't work! We add new parts and detail it, but it still doesn't work! We need a new vehicle. Or no vehicle at all in fact! For the past 12 years I have been deeply suspicious of any new method that comes down the pike, any new book that has the next best strategy. I always feel like a rabbit in *Watership Down*: I'm being baited with fresher carrots. That's all! Anyone with any common sense should be able to tell when they are being swindled. We all should be able to tell when we are being bamboozled.

No more strategies. No more visions. No more methods. No more renovations, customizations, and tweak jobs. Please! Jesus is not a supplement to boost my quality of life. He promises me death. And the life he does promise is not an enhanced life but a resurrected one, which is something totally other and probably beyond the domain of sensual experience. And this is what I'm holding out for.

10 Little Pieces of Advice to Take or Leave (July 7, 2008)

1. Lead leaderlessly. That is, lead in a non-leading kind of way. Serve. Step out of the leadership position continually. Perpetually. Create the vacuum for others to lead and serve.
2. Don't go anywhere. No goal. No destiny. No vision. Keep it real and keep it present. You either serve the vision or you serve the people.
3. Don't ever think of the "church" as some kind of entity ASIDE from the real flesh and blood people that constitute it. The church isn't the entity, even though it wants to be and constantly endeavors to be.
4. Allow worship and expression of all sorts to be indigenous. Never think of worship as instruction. It is God-ward, not human-ward.
5. If prayer is always in the form of a song and never said or read, so be it.
6. Allow freedom of expression, even if it's going to be weird, uncomfortable, and questionable. Judge it afterwards. Yes, when done with mutual respect, we do get used to this honest and authentic form of dialog and learning.
7. Let sinners play too.
8. Question everything.
9. Never be overly impressed with another person. No one is good but God alone.
10. Don't be afraid to kill the mood. Always be honest and free, no matter how uncomfortable you might cause others to feel.

Radical Grace and the Love of an Idea (August 22, 2008)

The most radical kind of grace is the kind that has no

expectations on the recipient. It loves and forgives before there is even a hint of worthiness or repentance. God doesn't love what I'm to become. He doesn't love the perfect idea or realization of David Hayward. He loves me as I am now. In fact, God loved me when I was dead, with nothing to offer and no hopes of offering anything back. This kind of radical grace, or love, is what the scriptures talk about.

Which is why it is just as important for me to love others in this way. It is completely expected for us to love those who show promise or from whom we can expect something back... even gratitude. But it is a radical kind of grace or love that loves and forgives without any hope of return. I reject the idea of loving someone because of their potential, or loving, forgiving or investing in the perfect idea of someone, my best idea of them. It is not remarkable to love someone because of what I hope they may become.

The same goes for the church. I refuse to love this community because of the potential it may have. It's not helpful to love them because I believe they are going to be great. I am to love them now. Like the father loved the prodigal son even before he had a chance to open his mouth and repent, I am to love my community as they are... while they are on the road without any hopes of reaching the destination. I am to love them now, as they actually are, with no hope of change or response. I am to love them without an eye on my hopes, dreams, visions or expectations of them. I don't love Rothesay Vineyard as an idea, but as they presently are.

Trapped or Free (September 11, 2008)

Are you feeling trapped? I suppose I could ask this of anybody in any kind of situation. Of course, I will add my disclaimer that there are some situations people find themselves in which they have no choice. They are indeed trapped and cannot escape. What I am addressing here is something different. And I guess I'm asking this particularly of pastors: Do you feel trapped? Let me tell you a story…

Lisa and I met in a Pentecostal bible college. We got married in 1980, moved to Boston for me to attend seminary. After I graduated we entered the Presbyterian church. Long story short, I was ordained in 1987 and started pastoring three Presbyterian churches in Atlantic Canada. I was, as some of my friends said, a strange mixture of reformed theology and charismatic experience. I tried and tried to inject some passionate, experiential type of worship and community life into the Presbyterian churches I pastored, but it was a long, arduous and painstaking process. I now question my attitude and the way I approached things back then. The gist is that over the five years I was in my first charge I experienced an intense frustration with the glacial progress of my intentions for the churches. This led to a deep feeling of thirst and longing for a passionate spirituality once again in my own personal and communal life.

Then, in 1993 I accepted an invitation by the Presbyterian Church in Canada to plant a church in the Annapolis Valley in Nova Scotia. They had done surveys and felt that there was the potential to have a Presbyterian church in that area. I accepted the invitation. I went with excitement, vision and hope. I could go into this virgin territory and start a new church with a clean slate and build the kind of church that I wanted. We moved there and started gathering people. At first I was thrilled. But it wasn't even a few months into it when I realized that it had fallen into the same rut I had been in for years before. One reason was that this new church plant attracted some lapsed Presbyterians in the area that were patiently waiting for a Presbyterian church to come, and they arrived with all their traditional Presbyterian expectations. Another reason is that the gravitational pull of any church is towards organization, stagnation and death, including this brand new baby church! I started having to deal with complaints about the music, the style of teaching, the money, the building, the people, the leaders… you name it. Overnight, it seemed, I had become a manager of bitter and difficult church-goers. But this happened to me and this church so quickly that I was overcome with despair. I started to even more seriously question my call as a pastor. I started looking around for options. But I had none. I started thinking about the possibility of becoming a full-time artist. But that was dreaming. What would I do for my family in the meantime? I read back in my journals from those days and they are full of questions, doubts, struggles, and depression. It stretched Lisa to the max and our marriage even further. What was I to do? I couldn't think of anything!

I remember one night going to bed early and lying there by myself in the dark. I started weeping. The tears rolled down my cheeks. I wasn't just unhappy. I was filled to the brim with a raw and hopeless despair I had never felt before. I could actually taste the bitter iron of sorrow on my tongue. I didn't know what to do. I didn't have any options. I was completely and hopelessly destined to fill out the rest of my sad days slaving in a job I hated and a church I couldn't stomach. I had no other choice but to finally admit: *I was trapped*.

That night I had a dream. This was all the dream was: I was like the prodigal son, returning from bondage to his home. And I heard the words, *"It's time!"*. That was it. I woke up at 5 a.m. filled with a joy like I'd never experienced before. I woke Lisa up and told her what happened. It was unbelievable. I was laughing! I woke up realizing that I wasn't trapped at all. I was a free man! I didn't have to do anything. And it wasn't just a cognitive thing. I *felt* free. What incredible happiness filled my mind and heart. I knew, immediately, that I was free and was free to leave. It didn't matter. I wasn't worried. Like the prodigal son, I could stay where I was and be satisfied with the bitter but secure food of my slavery, or I could leave all this and go. Just go! I told Lisa that I felt we should just quit. Why allow my comfortable salary with annual increases, my pension, my benefits, my position, to keep us enslaved? Why? Let's just leave! Let's just quit and see what happens! Do we trust God or not? We are free! Let's act like it!

Over the next couple of months we went through the whole process of telling our elders and the congregation, selling off our stuff and putting the rest in storage, and endlessly trying to explain our insanity to all those around us. No one understood. But we didn't care! We were free. We didn't have to remain enslaved. So we eventually packed up what we had left into our van and our utility trailer, buckled in our three young children, and drove away. We had never been happier. We had never been filled with more excitement or a sense of adventure. I dare say that the many months that followed were the most thrilling months of our lives. And I would do it all over again if it meant freedom for me and my family.

Perhaps you are feeling trapped where you are. Sometimes all it takes is the revelation that you are actually free. Sometimes it takes a revelatory peek into the reality of your situation to realize that you are actually not trapped. Sometimes the seduction of our securities is so powerful that it makes us think we are without options. Sometimes, when our securities and comforts are exposed as illusory, temporary and sometimes even as snares, we can free ourselves of them. This experience taught me that. It taught me that I am a free man, no matter what situation I find myself in. It is an incredibly liberating truth to know. It may not mean leaving the situation but living as a free person within it. But sometimes it may very well mean leaving the land of your slavery behind you and moving on to new and promised land that is waiting for you.

Spiritual Engineering (September 30, 2008)

I was skimming through a book on *Genocide*, by Alexander Laban Hinton. I'm fascinated by such topics because they expose the depravity of the human heart. Social engineering was the preoccupation of the Nazis, and this holds true for every other genocidal agenda.

Basically, social engineering intends to institute a new and better order. Genocide intends the design of the perfect society, and to implement this design through planned and consistent effort. The way this happens is two-fold: first, by facilitating the propagation of healthy stock, and two, by the containment or elimination of any disruptive factors.

I'm interested in how our designs for spiritual communities in many ways resemble genocidal intentions for society. How often have I been attracted to an alluring, charismatic and convincing personality who had an agenda to create and build a new kind of order? And how often have I witnessed and experienced the isolation and eventual separation and elimination of those who did not fit the program? I have to be even more honest than that: How often have I supported and even promoted these kinds of agendas to shape spiritual communities and the people within them?

This is a vital issue for me because I claim to be passionate about diversity in community. I argue that diversity is healthier than homogeneity for community life. I also insist that we must be brutally honest about what our intentions are for the community and the people within it. What are our designs for people? What plans do we have for them? How are we hoping to change them and shape them into the kind of community we want? Because the kind of community we want is going to determine what kind of plans, visions and goals we impose upon them. How much do our plans and intentions and designs violate who they already presently are? And is something already wrong with them that they need to be changed? Who is the judge of that? How do we treat people who will not or cannot comply with our wishes for them, no matter how good and noble our wishes might be?

These are important questions. If the church is to represent and actually be the vastly multifaceted and varietal diversity of the body of Christ, a body in which we cannot and are not to judge between the good and bad fish or the crops and the weeds, a body upon which we are not to call down fire from heaven to destroy the bad parts, then how does this determine the plans we have for this body? When we try to engineer the kind of community that we want, are we actually doing violence to the body of Christ and violating his parts?

My Policy is to Have No Policy (October 23, 2008)

I refuse to concoct plans for people's lives. I refuse to concoct a plan for the life of my church. I realize I'm going against the flow, like a salmon swimming up an impossible gush of watery onslaughts. But I just won't do it. So fire me!

I used to do it. I used to pray and wait and then articulate the vision and set out a one, three and five year plan with great gusto and with leadership and congregational support and fanfare. But I have stopped because I believe it destroys, in a violently sinister way, the lives of people and the life of a community. It's presumptuous and cruel and inhumane. I have been on the receiving end of this visionary kind of pogrom and I will no longer have any part of it. I realize how tantalizing, how dizzyingly intoxicating, visionary thinking and purpose-driven living can be. It tastes good, but it's poison.

There are many misconceptions out there. I recently met with a friend who is also a pastor who spoke about getting his people with the program in order to move the church forward. I told him that I didn't use that language or care for the community in that same way anymore. He saw the importance, he admitted, of just "being", but there has to be the "doing" too. I felt my temperature rise a little because I get this all the time. The presumption is that if you don't have a vision or a goal, then you just "be" and don't do anything. Or as someone else told me, "You just sit and wait by the phone for God to call." Of course he never does.

I have to clarify that this is erroneous thinking. Like my daughter, I have no plans for her life. I do father her in such a way that she may have the wherewithal to be a healthy, wise and confident woman. THAT will be her contribution to the world! Take care of the roots and the tree will bear fruit. And it will bear fruit in accordance with its unique kind. I pastor a community that I try to keep free of vision, goal-setting and agendas. That's my work for the most part. Many people now have grown an acute distaste for agendas on their lives. One such woman visited me earlier today and says that she can smell someone's plan for her life way down the road and avoids it like the plague because she sees it as soul-destroying. I think that is radically rebellious but radically healthy. Another salmon.

Ulterior Motives (October 24, 2008)

I speak and write frequently about being free of motive, or, in more vulgar terms, agenda, plan, vision, and goal. This is one of the most difficult concepts for us to understand, especially when we are in the people and religion business. So I want to share with you a quote:

*"The evangelicals I've felt the most fond of, the most comfortable around, and the most commonality with– regardless of political, social, or philosophical differences– were the ones who never tried to sell me on Jesus yet always seemed to be trying to live the life Jesus desired of them. The paradox of lifestyle evangelism is that while it might sound like a Christian's loving, friendly actions are all driven by an ulterior motive, in only **really** clicks when they're able to let go of that motive. The people who made the best case for Christianity were the ones who were genuinely unconcerned whether I ever decided to become a Christian or not."*

This was written by Daniel Radosh, a self-proclaimed Jewish agnostic, in his entertaining and enlightening book, *Rapture Ready: Adventures in the Parallel Universe of Christian Pop Culture*. Some might inquire: *"But Jesus told us to go into all the world and make disciples!"* I think we need to understand what this means on a deeper level. Only those who either don't care **or** who have a foundational grasp of and a thorough trust in the sovereignty of God, the universality of his love, grace and forgiveness, and the reconciliation of all things, can drop ulterior motives in living with and loving others.

Separation (November 7, 2008)

Yesterday Lisa and I were in a business being helped by a young woman. We really liked her. She had a sweet spirit, was very helpful, kind and engaging. After a while, she noticed on the forms that I was a pastor. She was happy about that and quietly let us know that she was a believer too. She began talking to us about how difficult she found it being a Christian in her work environment. She struggles. She shared her experiences with her own church, other Christians, and the churches in the area and how divisive they are. She asked me questions about our church, our worship style and all that. I really enjoyed our conversation. It was, I think, a mutually encouraging encounter. We even talked about getting together with her and her husband because, being new to the area, they would like to have more fellowship with other Christians.

But the whole time we were talking I had this knot growing in my gut. Her theological and ecclesiastical position was obviously more conservative than mine. I could tell by the way she talked that she was used to a more traditional expression of Christianity and was comfortable with that. I don't mind that at all. That wasn't the issue. The issue was that I was concerned that she was going to find out about me, my blog, my cartoons, my theological position, my history and the history of my church. Stained and blemished at least! I was worried that she would find me and my church scandalous and wouldn't want to associate with me anymore.

This kind of tension always brings me back to Paul's wisdom in Romans 14:10:

Why do you pass **judgment** on your brother or sister? Or you, why do you **despise** your brother or sister?

The judgment comes from those who think they are holier than others, live more righteous lives and are more pure than their sinfully compromised brothers and sisters. The despising comes from those who think they are more developed, advanced and mature, beyond the law and freed from traditions and regulations. This is the problem with the Christian community and even the spiritual- or faith-community in general... conservatives who judge liberals and liberals who despise conservatives. This is the problem! We are either perpetuating this terrible cycle of division or we are victims of it. Often both!

This discomfort I felt while talking with this wonderful woman probably tells more about me than her. But my feelings aren't unfounded. It has happened to me many, many times. I love fellowship with Christians different than I and work hard to create that kind of diverse environment within our community. But my experience has generally been that many Christians, usually more conservative ones, prefer to separate themselves from me and my kind.

Differences, Dissent and Division (December 16, 2008)

I haven't written in a while. I'm sorry. Maybe you're not. I would like to write more often. I do have people insisting that I should just shut up and draw. My cartoons and my art says enough, they say. Perhaps my art and cartoons are incarnational. After all, the Word did become flesh. But that flesh did speak. So I think words are sometimes necessary. Like St. Francis of Assisi said, *"Preach the gospel always. If necessary use words."* So today is one of those days when I feel I need to write something.

I've been reading some theology lately. Doped up following my nose surgery has lent itself to metaphysical thinking. I'm still slightly dopey. My mornings are okay, but as the day progresses my head begins to pound right behind my nose and eyes until the point of exhaustion. I pop some pills and that helps, theologically speaking.

I've met recently with a couple of friends who have left the local church and the faith as well. I love them, totally respect them, and listen hard to what they are saying. I'm interested in what they are reading and what they believe now. I'm fascinated by it. I think it is important for me to listen to what they believe and why. I think it is crucial to listen to what Hitchens and Harris and Dawkins are saying. I think it is necessary for me to listen to what science is saying. Evolutionists. Mystics. New Agers. Universalists. Syncretists. Neo-Gnostics. Everyone.

You know, in the earliest church, the Fathers contested with people with differing views as though they were a diverse and dissenting part of the larger community. I think, for instance, Irenaeus, when he challenged the Gnostics, betrayed a humble deference toward them. At the earliest point there was no clear line of division that separated the "heretics" from the "orthodox". This came later with the councils and creeds. They mingled together in the same communities and churches. I personally think it is important to work towards a clear theology. Faith seeks understanding. But I also believe it is important and even required by charity to permit all voices an audience and to see all people and opinions as typical of a diverse community striving towards love and health.

When you think of it, when Paul said in the Corinthian correspondence that one prophet should speak; then when another stands up to speak the first one should be quiet and sit down; and that the content of what they say is held up to scrutiny, discerned and judged by the community... wasn't Paul implicitly giving room for heresy? The root of heresy literally means an opinion that is contrary to another. Later it came to mean a belief that is contrary to the orthodox doctrine or the most popularly held opinion. I think we need to listen to more apparently "heretical" views because I personally believe that much of what is popularly held as true is in fact false and needs to be challenged by opposing views.

And, as Forrest said, *"That's all have to say about that."*

Dietrich Bonhoeffer Block Print (January 21, 2009)

I've begun working on a series of theologians in block-print. This is technically my first one, although I have an image of Karl

Barth prepared for carving and printing. This one is of the

German theologian Dietrich Bonhoeffer. It is interesting to me that I am releasing this while the Tom Cruise film *Valkyrie* is making its rounds. The common theme of course is the plot to kill Hitler.

But that's not why I admire Bonhoeffer. I love his little book *Life Together*. I read it every now and again to remind myself of the importance of community and how to protect it from the ambitious agendas of this world, both religious and secular. It reminds me that community is not created by the proper application of technique and vision. Here's just one quote that cuts to the marrow:

Every human wish dream that is injected into the Christian community is a hindrance to genuine community and must be banished if genuine community is to survive. He who loves his dream of a community more than the Christian community itself becomes a destroyer of the latter, even though his personal intentions may be ever so honest and earnest and sacrificial.

The community I am a part of and oversee tries to remember this and live by it. We try to remember that what we have, if we "have" it at all, is a gift. It is something to be cherished, protected and enjoyed. We didn't create it. We can't sustain it. We can't guarantee its future. It seems to be totally out of our hands, while at the same time we are somehow responsible for its care.

Gays Go! (January 27, 2009)

Last night I had a very disturbing dream. In my dream there are many lesbians as a part of our community. In fact, it looks like the entire cast of the television show, The L Word. They are my dear friends, brothers and sisters of mine that I love and enjoy. But the disturbing part is when they decide they have to leave. They find that the institution is becoming increasingly unfriendly, unkind and adversarial for them, and that they feel they have no choice, really, but to leave. Well, they do have a choice: stay if you promise to change into something else, or leave if you won't. I feel as though I must stay behind in order to encourage and nurture an inclusive community of love, so their departure feels permanent and painful. I weep with deep sorrow and wake up crying.

I immediately realize that this doesn't just apply to gays, but to all kinds of people because of race, creed, religion, social status, economics, and even personality types. The lesbians in my dream represent, for me, all those who must continually struggle within community because they are different. They not only have to fight for a place, but for their basic rights. I long to experience a community of broad diversity, and it seems increasingly impossible to realize. Of course, this must have been what, in part, inspired today's cartoon.

magic, tricks and wishful thinking (January 29, 2009)

Some people treat the book as though it were some kind of ancient document of magical formulas. Just believe in a correct way, speak things in a proper way, and all your wishes will come true. When I watch what happens on television and in some books I read, I sometimes feel like I'm at a magic show. Smoke and mirrors. Have you read Joan Didion's book, The Year of Magical Thinking? Her husband suddenly dies, and she realizes that the following year was a year of thinking magically. That is… she realizes in her own self-analysis that she catches herself believing that if a person hopes for something enough or performs the right actions that an unavoidable event can be averted or something good can happen that one wishes for. I hear her! An analogy, in many ways, for many things. Silly rabbit! Tricks are for kids!

Cultural Legacy and Mitigated Speech (February 21, 2009)

I just finished reading Malcolm Gladwell's *Outliers*. It is a fascinating read. Basically, his thesis is that what makes a person succeed is not necessarily or only his or her ingenuity, energy, determination, or vision, but a series of events and

legacies that this person is given. A great deal depends on chances this person is offered and takes. In other words, Gladwell is talking about the importance of our communities on whether we fail or succeed.

The chapter I found the most intriguing was about plane crashes. Briefly, it has been concluded that most plane crashes are not because of one catastrophic problem, but the accumulation of smaller ones. It is also concluded that the more people are actively involved in the flight of the plane, from the captain to the first officer to the flight engineer to the flight attendants, the fewer accidents occur. So, when little problems occur, many eyes and hands are on deck to help solve these issues. If these are managed, accidents will be diverted. So, it is a community effort that ensures the safety of the flight. It is absolutely critical, therefore, that there is clear communication between the flight crew when problems arise. It is a community effort that gives the captain and the airline an accident-free career.

In the nineties, Korea Air had so many plane crashes that it lost its status as an airline. A professional researched the problem and discovered that the culprit was "mitigated speech", that is, downplaying or sugarcoating the meaning of what is being said. Because of the Koreans' deep and traditional respect for authority, subordinate flight crew-members would never ever try to instruct, correct or challenge a flight crew member higher up the rungs of authority. Once mitigated speech was corrected, Korea Air rebounded and became the respected airline it is today.

It seems that flight crew-members today are trained on how to communicate clearly what they mean. There are precise levels of urgency and clarity. Also, it's best for the first officer to fly the plane with the captain in the co-pilot's seat. That way the captain feels comfortable challenging the first officer if something goes wrong. And everyone on the flight crew has authority when they notice a problem arise. Plus, everyone speaks to each other on a first name basis, avoiding labels that carry the intimidating weight of authority. Even those who have the cultural legacy of unquestioning respect for authority learn to divest themselves of this during training. Korean pilots are now among the most respected and accident-free in the world.

If we are as concerned about the "safety" of the people within our communities, then I find Gladwell's insights applicable. The

church has a cultural legacy of deep respect towards authority. When I came to this church from the Presbyterian, I moved from an ecclesiastical authority structure to a personal authority structure that is just as dangerous. Authority, authority, authority... I hear it all the time. The religious cultural legacy I come from demands that I not question authority. And it makes me wonder if this is the cause of so many fatal church accidents. Many become proficient at mitigated speech for fear of not just challenging authority, but even upsetting authority or hurting it's feelings! It has taken me years, with limited success, to work against this unhealthy and even dangerous deference to authority. I think if we want to see religious communities succeed, we'd be wise to apply a few principals:

1. No more mitigated speech. When it comes to the health of the community, direct communication matters. Enable people to mean what they say and say what they mean without fear of repercussions.
2. Empower others to fly. Decentralize power and decision-making. Share the welfare of the community.
3. Everyone on a first name basis. Remove all residue from former authoritative paradigms. Today, a lot of what is called post-modern or emergent is basically cooler and hipper mutations of our old accident-prone structures.
4. If you've ever sat by the emergency exit on a flight, you know you are essentially emergency staff if a problem occurs. So... teams! Everyone is involved! Everyone can, if they wish, participate in the health and welfare of the community.

No one dares say anything. That's why there's silence as it crashes!

Fruit in a Barren Land (February 25, 2009)

I met with a good friend today who is a member of our community. I was sharing with her what I was feeling these days with people who've left, who've decreased their level of support, and who've pulled back in some way or another. I told her I find it hard to be optimistic in the face of such loss. It doesn't seem to matter how hard I try or work, it's like I'm carrying a leaky pail.

©nakedpastor

"Pastor, we're really getting tired of doing this!"

She admitted to me that she would like to be a part of a success story just once. All the effort that goes into doing the things we do at the grassroots level is just that: grassroots. It's meaningful, but small. There's no wave of people coming. There's no fanfare. No recognition. There's no measurable gain that we can enjoy. Although everything we do we do with a clear conscience, certain that we are to be who we are and doing what we do, there's never any marked victory. Sure, we sold land and paid off our debt. But this doesn't measure the health or success of our community. In fact, it could very well affect it adversely. But I know what she means. I've often wondered why, in spite of our constant efforts to be and do good, there's no profitable gain from it. I want to be a part of a success story too. I would love to be presently rewarded. But no! We aren't and I'm not sure we ever will be.

(*Pull the camera back for wide-angle shot*): This very desire... to be a part of a success story... is the problem! It blinds us to the present. It pollutes our thoughts and actions with ambitious desires for a lofty goal, the fulfillment of our visions and dreams that have been fabricated in our discontented hearts. It also blinds us to the subtle rewards we do enjoy that can't be calculated. Are we content to be and do good and leave the results up to the Other? We can plant. We can water. We can tend. But the increase is a gift.

Sterilizing the Body (February 26, 2009)

I'm warning you that if you want to have a relational community, a community of friends, a community where people are free to be authentic, honest and open, a community where there's a collegial effort to share the gathering times, then you are in for chaos! It's going to be messy. I promise!

It's not going to be messy for a couple of reasons. One is that you will inevitably have a collection of diverse individuals that are full of surprises... some welcome, some not. But then again, it depends who you are. More about that in a sec. For instance, because my messages aren't packaged presentations but more conversational in nature, sometimes someone will say something that will totally derail the discussion with some whacky idea. But then again, it depends who you are. But more about that in a sec. Or, if someone decides they'd like to try out the tambourine during the singing but don't have a lick of rhythm, you have to deal with the sometimes humorous embellishments to the music. But then again, it depends who you are. But more about that in a sec. Or, sometimes during the singing, someone might feel he has something important to share with the community, so he comes up and dominates the stage for a while, sometimes killing the vibe that has been built over the last several minutes with just the right music. But then again, it depends who you are. But more about that in a sec.

But the other reason why it is going to be messy is that it depends on who you are. Some people don't mind the intellectual derailments, preferring diversity of opinion or

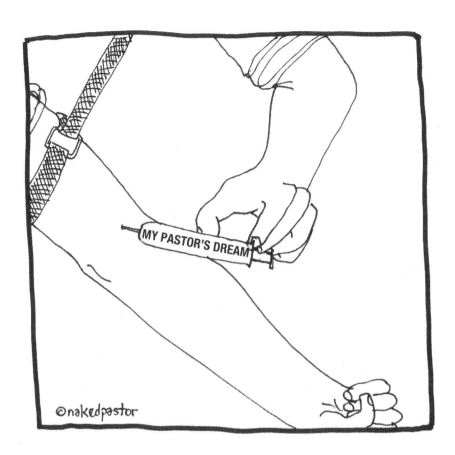

enjoying the fact that the authoritative voice (*mine*) can be challenged or complimented or changed. Some people don't notice the off-beat tambourine because they don't have rhythm themselves, or it's their son, or they love the fact that the band, which used to be elitist, is just that unrestricted now. Some people appreciate the people who sometimes dominate the stage and share what's on their hearts because they are more emotionally expressive than I am, or they actually do happen to be in touch with issues that are current in peoples' lives and address these with edifying words. But not everybody appreciates these things all of the time. Including me!

You see, in all these cases (and these kinds of things happen *all the time* in our community) these things only wreck the mood if

I have an agenda I am trying to fulfill, a goal I am trying to reach, a vision I am trying to materialize. The problem with my philosophy (and most people in our community agree with this): *everybody* can play, is (and this is where people have issues): *anybody* can play. I could sterilize Sunday morning to where the singers lead their part with explicit instructions to the community that they are not to interfere. Then I can get up and speak with the firm understanding that I alone am permitted to speak uninterrupted. But then, we wouldn't be who we are, would we? But my, it would be cleaner!

What if the point of community was just to be community that is working towards being a functional, healthy and whole community, a small model of what unity in diversity looks like, a local expression of the Body with all its members? What if the whole point was to appreciate the diversity, encourage it, nurture it and practice it, in spite of our personal preferences, opinions and tastes? Although I'm convinced that this is true, I'm still not sure it is possible.

A Brooding Peace (March 10, 2009)

There is a lot on my mind, and I'm reading some good material on and by Wendell Berry. I've always appreciated what he has to say. To be honest, I'm feeling rather tranquil. In the midst of all the pressure of this world and my community, I'm feeling calm. However, I do feel the weight of temptation to succumb to the vision-casting, goal-setting and energy-boosting climate I find myself in. Even in my community, there is always the seduction to hype things up. It is difficult to be content with the small things... that is, contentment, love, relationships, serving, helping, peace. These are hard work that our zeal can distract us from.

Systems and Power (March 31, 2009)

I just finished reading Garrow's massive biography of Martin Luther King, Jr., *Bearing the Cross*. Garrow is a great writer to be able to link together so many dates, events, and people in such a gripping and moving story.

One of King's leaders, Jim Bevel, summarized what he felt were the four major forces that kept the ghetto in place:

1. lack of economic power;
2. political disenfranchisement;
3. lack of knowledge and information; and
4. lack of self-respect and self-dignity among the people of the ghetto.

He concluded that the project had to create enough self-dignity and self-respect in the people of the ghetto so that they will not tolerate the inhumane system under which they are now forced to live, and will replace it with a community of love.

Bevel recommended to the leadership that they focus first on number one. His reason for advising this was because he believed that:

You fight a machine by making people grow so that they don't fit into the machine anymore.

It struck me how King's movement began with energy, zeal, vision and hope, but gradually ground to a slow and depressing struggle with small victories. The story again impressed me with how humanity has the uncanny ability to resist change by adopting manifold methods of entrenchment... anything from physical violence to empty promises to just plain refusal. King came to the conclusion late in his career that he was no longer interested in seeking integration into the present value structure. He realized that the structure itself was the problem and needed to be radically changed. The evil was systemic and not just personal. He even recommended some kind of modified socialism. Some believe this, and not the civil rights movement, is what got him killed.

We often face institutional power gone bad or systemic evil, as well as those who manage it. I found the four forces insightful. These four forces can be seen as stages for us to go through: self-respect to knowledge to shared power to equality. It is important and necessary for people everywhere to grow in their self-respect and dignity so that they cannot be controlled by these powers. New wine bursts old wineskins. Changed people conquer the principalities and powers that would enslave us. Even the ones we are comfortable with.

10 Survival Tips (May 5, 2009)

I think all religious communities, like our earth, are on a collision course with their demise. And it's our own fault, not the "world's". I've been mulling some thoughts around. If we are going to survive into the future, our communities need to:

1. get and stay **small** (like the best farms);
2. be **autonomous** but accountable to other communities (like tribes);
3. be **indigenous** in expression (local creativity and freedom of expression);
4. see **love** as the new hermeneutic of our books (instead of obedience, justification, salvation, etc.);
5. reject even the subtlest forms of **coercion** (no imposed agendas);
6. abandon **visionary** thinking (love without the oppression of expectations);
7. cultivate **thinkers** who explore the reconciliation of all things (global intelligence);
8. commit to **long-term** or even life-long oversight (relationship);
9. build an attitude of **resistance** to success-story thinking (anti-pop);
10. **engage** all sciences, religions and philosophies with an open, compassionate and humble mind (dialogue).

And that's just the beginning.

One Flew Over the Church's Nest (May 13, 2009)

I have visited insane people before. I have visited insane members of my church who have been admitted to the hospital's psyche ward. I have been insane myself. I am familiar with its geography.

One time I visited a lady who believed that the reason the nurses were taking blood was because there was gold in her veins. She honestly believed that the medical staff was mining for gold every time they took her blood, and that they were getting rich off of her. She also told me that God told her this. Then God told her that she was receiving divine guidance in spite of her imprisonment. I met her friends one day. They were all pretty much the same. They had visions, dreams, and frequent communications from God. They were emotionally or mentally ill. I understood that. Most of them didn't. There was no way I would say, *"You're crazy! You're out of your mind! Get a grip! Geez! Do you realize where you are?"* Instead, like a good visitor, I would sit and listen to them, nodding my head in feigned agreement. I didn't want to hurt them. I didn't want to hinder their healing process. It wasn't time to confront and challenge. It was time to just be with them and help them feel loved and affirmed. Besides, even if I did challenge them, they would only think I was crazy… another patient.

Sometimes I feel church is like that. Sorry. I do. Sometimes we are all talking like, *"God told me this. God told me that. I saw this. I saw that. This is what's really happening, etc., etc."* We come up with such incredible and even outlandish ideas and theories and predictions. Often I catch myself nodding my head in feigned agreement because I don't want to hurt that person's feelings. Granted, they do the same to me. Sometimes I think

A metaphor for a pastor attempting to control the people.

what people are saying is absolute nonsense, but I'll never tell them that. Besides, I've come to learn that we will believe what we are going to believe unless something profoundly traumatic happens to us to challenge our preconceived notions. We are all walking around in an insane asylum believing our own delusions, thinking everybody but me is crazy, and waiting for the right person to come along to swallow my story and advocate for me. We are delusional. Like the best of religions insist: illusion is the air we breathe.

Sorry, it's not a pretty or upbeat picture. But that's what I'm feeling these days about the business of religion, spirituality and the church. It's insane. It's like *One Flew Over the Church's Nest*. The best we can do is keep out Nurse Cratchit!

Defiance (May 14, 2009)

I appreciated the film *Defiance* because it reminded me of our community. Not that we are under severe persecution and are operating underground. But in the face of incredible odds, we are surviving as a community. That's what I'm talking about.

The main task of the Bielski brothers isn't to form an army to attack the Nazi forces. Their main job, overall, is to maintain their small and harassed community, to keep it safe, protected, fed, sheltered and unified. More than that, they somehow have to try to keep hope alive in the afflicted people. Every once in a while new refugees wander into the camp for shelter and they were quickly integrated into the safety of the community. Their defiance is not as much against the Nazis, a nation or a people, but against death itself, against annihilation, against division, against hopelessness, against fear. Tuvia's defiance represents his unwillingness to surrender to the manifest destiny of the powers towards world domination and of his own people towards extermination. The film focuses on the inner tensions of the forest dwelling refugees and Tuvia's constant endeavor to maintain morale in a community so harassed. Their occasional raids on Germans and their collaborators is the side story.

Last Sunday when we called all the mothers up to receive some flowers, my heart sank. I was overcome by how many of them have gone through and are going through incredible suffering. The men seated out there behind them were just as much in pain. The stories! And I realized that what we need most is to keep our community as healthy as possible. Our defiance is not so much against everything "out there", but more against our fears, our hopelessness, and against death itself. These people need to know that they are cared for here, loved, protected, and provided for. No, we're not isolationist or protectionist. We welcome any who wander into our camp. We are like refugees who have discovered a safe place to find faith, joy, love, and hope, and to keep ourselves alive. It is a place to survive and even thrive together. To me, the fact that we are such a community is our testimony.

Fantasy Fantastic Communities (June 3, 2009)

I am a part of a stubborn community of people. But I'm thankful for that. It is partially because of our stubbornness that we are still here. But I'm thankful for it for another, more important, reason: they will not be coerced into doing something they don't want just to fulfill some expectation, no matter how virtuous or noble.

The pressure to envision the community as something better or even other than what it is inescapable and constant. My community, however, demands to be recognized and appreciated for what it is. For who they are! I always compare it to a loving relationship. If I constantly want my wife to look like Angelina Jolie, have sex with me every day, and worship the ground I walk on, then my expectations are eventually going to kill me and her. I will resent the fact that my fantasies are never fulfilled, and she will resent the fact that she herself is never loved. We will end up in divorce court because I refuse to see her, respect her and love her as she is, and she refuses to conform to my fantasies of my imaginary her.

I almost daily have to purge my mind of expectations, objectives, dreams, visions, goals and fantasies about my community or it will destroy me with disappointment, resentment and bitterness. The same for the community! If they constantly feel like they are never measuring up to my dreams for them, it will end in disaster. But the temptation is real because this is precisely how I was trained to oversee communities! This is how almost every community functions. And it is killing people and community. To unconditionally love these people as they are and this community as it is… that's my commitment.

Family Circle (June 4, 2009)

Hey! I just came up with an idea: How about all churches commit to a one-year moratorium on vision-casting, goal-setting, and mission statements? All the people I've talked with who are involved with these kinds of things admit, some to their shame, that they are completely useless undertakings anyway. Many I've talked to admit that once they come up with a firm vision statement, it is immediately made obsolete by some totally unforeseen issue or event or just the plain unwillingness of the people to be herded into the thin corridor of compromise, sacrifice and conformity that leads to the death of the human spirit! Sometimes I think that working on these vision-statements make us feel like we are important and doing something significant, when all we are doing is playing with language, teasing our members, and flirting with disaster.

Today I met with atheists. A few friends of mine, who used to be faithful members of our community, invited me to meet over beer. Individually! Synchronicity or what?! One of them used to be a very faithful and involved member. Then he went through a "crisis", and decided at the end of it that he was an atheist. He wanted to tell me that he was thankful that none of the members of my community ever pressured him in what he believed. He thought it was commendable that he was allowed to conclude what he concluded and still remain friends with these people. He thought it was noteworthy that these people would rather remain his friend than his ideological co-signer. I realized that many might think this was a failure on the part of my community to challenge this guy and direct him back to the way. Not him. He thought it was something I should be proud of... that the people of this community allowed people the freedom to be who they were and believe what they believed. Or didn't believe. Whatever terminology you want to use.

I wonder what would happen if we universally decided to no longer embrace the whole goal-setting culture. What if we decided, instead, to just gather, like a family, and love each other and be openly welcoming to guests as well as those who would like to be adopted into our kin?

Frank Viola and Re-Imagining (July 3, 2009)

I attended Frank Viola's *Re-Imagining the Church* conference held just outside Toronto, Ontario, Canada, in my hometown of Newmarket, last weekend. I took advantage of it being there and had the opportunity to visit my family. I want to thank Frank for personally inviting me. Even though I am not directly involved with the house-church movement that he espouses, he still thought it would be worth my while to attend. And it was. I'm glad I went. I want to try to articulate a few observations I made about the conference. Please forgive the fact that this is not a professionally written essay, but a quickly jotted observation I wish to share with you.

It was sold out with 200 registered. It took place in a very comfortable, plush sanctuary with state-of-the-art audio-visual equipment. We were seated at large round tables with approximately 10 people per table. I didn't know anyone. It was a little awkward for me, but I sat at a table and introduced myself as best I could. I made an effort to say hi to Frank since he was so kind to invite me. We'd never met except online. I've received some free copies of his books and reviewed one or two on this blog. He is very friendly, kind and has a warm sense of humor. Viola is obviously passionate about Jesus and his body, the church. There were a couple of times I felt like I was at a good ol' Pentecostal revival meeting. I admired his passion and his zeal for the church. I also admired... and I told him this... his team of several men who showed incredible comraderie with Frank. I told him it must be wonderful to have such a group of strong supporters with him at all times. He agreed. I think that shows wisdom. It also shows that he is a team player, and that is often a good thing.

Something happened to me that was both uncomfortable and humorous. At one point we were to go around the table and introduce ourselves and talk about our own story with house-church. They started to my right and went around the table, so I was the last one. They talked about their negative experiences in the institutional church and how they were either trying to find a house fellowship to be a part of, or trying to start a house fellowship, or being involved in one already. They talked of the benefits of not having authority figures, hierarchical leadership, brick and mortar buildings, paid staff, set meeting times, impersonal services, and all the rest. They had success stories of how things were going in their house-churches. Then it got

to me. I said, *"Well, I feel very much like a fish out of water here, but not only do I go to an institutional church... I pastor one!"* *"Oh!"* some said, *"They're okay. They're fine! In fact, I got saved in one!"* Etc., etc. It was both cute and funny. (Just on a side

note, I think I detected in the voice of many people the need for legitimization. That's one problem with the house-church movement. It is still in its early stages, and because of the lingering entrenchment of institutional Christianity, most house-churches seem to struggle with feeling illegitimate, disconnected from the "real" church. Just a thought.)

The truth is, I've been a part of house churches or house fellowships or whatever you want to call them, as well as the institutional church. In my opinion, you just need to pick which pan you want to fry in. The house-churches have their own peculiar problems just like institutional churches do. But, more importantly, I think both struggle with much of the same issues: power struggles, the prevalence of the principalities and powers, locale, time, relational conflict, authenticity, realness, commitment, money, and the rest. In fact, one gentleman gave a presentation of his desire to start a network of house-churches because there is strength, security and safety in numbers. In my mind that is just another way of saying movement or denomination or fellowship. He's right but he's talking denominationalism in its earliest stages.

The moment you have any expectations at all on others as a group, especially in the interest of that group, you have the inception of institutionalism. If you don't want an Institution or an Organization, then you can have no expectation at all on others. None at all! Not monetary, moral, missional, or any other kind. No expectations or desires whatsoever. We find that impossible because of the style religion has morphed into today and which we have wholeheartedly adopted. I think true freelancing is excellent, but it is extremely rare. I think institutions can be good. But the effort it takes to fight for an institution's continued liberation from the principalities and powers is so arduous that very, very few are willing to acquire it.

Viola says that he has been outside of the institutional church for over 20 years. But the problems that he admits so beset the house-church movement sound remarkably similar to what, say, my denomination, the Vineyard movement, presently struggles with. The issues of theology, purity, passion, mission, power and authority, money, commitment, isolation versus networking and clustering, are identical. We are all talking about the same old solutions to the same old problems. So, if I were Frank Viola, this is what I would be struggling with:

First of all, decide what you want to be: institution or not. Like there is no 'kind of pregnant', there is no 'kind of church'. You either are or you aren't an institution. I'm married. Marriage is an institution. It can't be helped. Lisa's and my struggle is how to be in loving commitment without falling prey to the dangers of institutionalism, or just being bound by a legal contract rather than love. So, if they decide not to be institutional, then forget trying to organize, inspire, or motivate groups of people according to a particular vision or goal. I realize that all of Viola's fears would come rushing in: heresy or just plain theological silliness, power-struggles and abuses, drifting away from the biblical Jesus and faith, lone-rangers and maverick leadership, cultism, and a complete lack of control over what's going on in people's living rooms.

However, if he is willing to become institutional (which I think he needs to if he wants his passions to bear fruit), then I would say this: I think Viola and company just need to admit that they are a church-planting movement and get on with it. Now, from my observation, all of the people at my table were people who have left the institutional church with unsavory memories of it. I totally understand that and don't judge that at all. I believe them. But Viola should realize that his primary mission field is people who have left the institutional church and are looking for a way to fellowship with other believers in a safer, more authentic, and more biblical way. There was talk about saving the lost too, but this is obviously secondary because it is the found that finds them. I know many, many people who've left the institutional church, so the mission field is huge and the harvest is ripe! Some are ex-pastors too, so there are teachers out there looking for an audience. I suspect this will focus their efforts to accomplish their dreams and also give the people joining a feeling of legitimacy, that they are still somehow connected to the historic, holy, catholic church and not on some cosmic cult ride. Of course, having said this, it creates the problems Viola is trying to avoid, like structure, organization, hierarchy, trained and educated leadership, control, financial need, etc.

These are just some of the things I would say. I like Frank and think he's on to something. I admire his zeal. Frank works hard to inspire others to find their original passion for Jesus again, their first love, or else it is all just a game. But many times I had the impression that they were fighting hard against being something that they already are... the church. They are just the church like it has always been since its birth. They are just the church in new, and some would say biblical clothes. No. They've just rearranged the furniture, but the house is the same. It's just a matter of style. My church works hard to be "organic", "authentic" and "biblical", and yet we are very institutional. Can't be helped.

Like Frank said, *"There is just one church!"* Exactly! We may look different, but we are brothers from the same mother.

old cartoon revisited: visionary veggies (July 15, 2009)

VISION CASTING

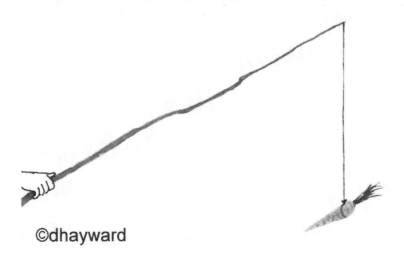

©dhayward

This is a cartoon I posted last year. It's one of my favorites. I think visionary thinking is pretty useless and sometimes even violent. I consider vision-casting as mostly a group exercise in futility. It is like putting the carrot in front of the horse to get it to go in your desired direction. I have been the one holding the stick. I relinquish that now. I've also been the one trying to attain that elusive carrot. It's plastic. And once you've achieved it, if you ever do, you have to start all over again. Okay, okay, okay… for those of you who insist one cannot live without vision and that I do have a vision and won't admit it… here's my vision: my vision is to have no vision.

Just a Few Random Thoughts (July 24, 2009)

1. People don't change their minds. Only rarely! Transformation is not a desirable option to our brains. It seems to require trauma, the threat of imminent death,

to provoke real change of mind and bring about true transformation. Is it possible to enter death and be transformed while we are alive?

2. The greatest enemy of community is fantasy... visionary and wishful thinking. The lack of gratitude for what is, the unwillingness to appreciate what is, or the disdain for what is, erodes the fabric of community. Can we love unconditionally without coercion?

3. Our gross naiveté about the principalities and powers and their persistent desire and ability to enslave groups and individuals perpetuates the abuses institutions, including the church, are notorious for. Can all people be free?

4. Avoid naysayers as well as yes-men. You can always find complainers to agree with you. You can always find encouragers to agree with you. Can we find the courage to form our own minds independently, wisely, and compassionately?

5. Listen to what the atheists are saying about the non-provability of God; discern the Christ-Principle in all things; have compassion for all beings. Is it possible to see all things as being reconciled?

Come In and Go Out (October 7, 2009)

More people leave our church. I have a gift. It's obvious. I can't hold people in a community. Sometimes I feel it is my fault. Sometimes I actually wonder if I should throw in the towel and let the church get a real pastor. Then, sometimes, when I'm feeling less insecure, I realize that when people gather on their own volition there are no guarantees about stability. Just today I was talking with one of our community. She was wondering if there's some kind of spirit in our church that's been here ever since the split back in 1997... that somehow our body got a spirit of division, like HIV... always there waiting to manifest itself when the body is weak. These "spirits" we talk about, in my opinion, can be chalked up to character issues in our own hearts and minds.

I realize too that I don't help matters. If I had a charismatic personality, was a motivational speaker, kept the ship running tightly, was orthodox, held to traditional morality and adhered to the middle road of evangelical conservativism... you know: like a regular pastor, then we'd probably hold our ground and even grow.

But... I was called an anomaly again just yesterday. Because I'm unwilling to pretend to be something I'm not. Thing is, I respect this same sentiment in others. Now that's a huge problem. But doesn't this have something to do with love... the love I live in and am given, and the love I give? I can't see it any other way. We are free to come and go. We are free to go in and come out and find pasture. But I miss every one of them that go.

Structure and Authenticity (October 18, 2009)

Some people have been visiting our church lately. Checking us out. One of the comments I get is that they just love the authenticity that they feel. They see that people are really free to be who they are without fear of judgment. They get the sense that they are allowed to explore their own spiritual paths and discover their own ways of living out their faith. Some say that they are just searching and don't want to make any commitments in any direction, and they get the feeling that they are allowed to do that here in the context of a supportive, caring community who are partners in pilgrimage with them. They hint that they might keep trying us out.

So we'll see. My experience is that those with a long history in the faith or in the church won't last as long because, even though they love the raw, real authenticity, at some point they want to see expressions of spiritual authority, direction, vision, goals, structure, and some kind of a moral standard. Searching for the perfect church, they think they've found the solution to their disappointing church experience from the past. But when they begin to realize that they've only found the opposite of their previous church experience, then they think that adding structure, authority and higher moral standards to this out of control congregation would make this authentic church experience better.

They are wrong. You can't have both. You can't have authority, vision, goals, structures, and higher moral standards along with raw authenticity. You can't. You have to choose. You can't manage people and expect them to feel free. You can't cast vision for a community and expect people to feel independent and autonomous. You can't govern people's ideas and lifestyles and expect them to feel self-directed. You can't establish some kind of moral standard and expect people not to feel judged when they don't or can't comply. You can't lead people in a certain direction and expect them to feel free to explore their own paths.

The wineskin story applies. Some desire new wine, but they might want it in the hardened, crusty leather of the old wineskins. Won't happen. New wine requires new, supple leather that expands and stretches and moves in all kinds of ways. And this unpredictable, loose, unmanageable kind of non-structure is undesirable for many.

Agendaless Sanctuary (October 20, 2009)

My agenda is to have no agenda. This frustrates so many people, including myself. But I resist the temptation, and I have to resist every day. It seems that the most natural thing to do when people gather together is to try to manage them.

It may not be the most natural but it seems to be the most immediate. The zealots, the religious, the spiritual, the leaders, the authorities, the professionals, would like to see the people (for their own good, of course) follow a prescribed but kindly path to a better life that they envision for them. I understand this. I totally get it.

I live in a world inundated with agenda. I am daily assaulted by millions of agendas aimed at capturing my imagination, my passion, my commitment, my allegiance, my money, my body, my soul. It is relentless and exhaustive. So, why not provide at least one place in the world where we leave agenda outside the door? Why not provide a place, like our homes and families ought to be, where people can enter without any fear of being marketed, analyzed, polled, compared, solicited or persuaded?

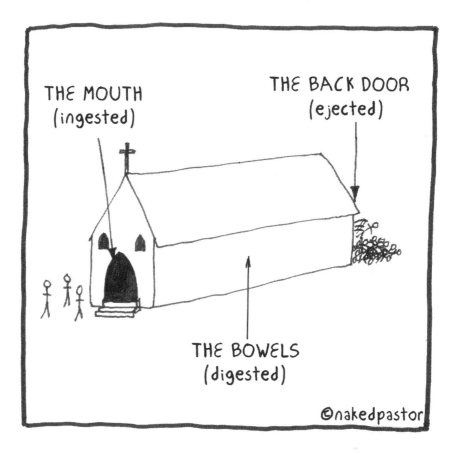

THE MOUTH
(ingested)

THE BACK DOOR
(ejected)

THE BOWELS
(digested)

©nakedpastor

And... I have an idea... why don't we call this place a *sanctuary*: a place of refuge and safety from agendas, goals, visions and purposes? I don't care what kind of liturgy it is... from the highest with bells and smells to the lowest with circles of silence. It doesn't matter. And I don't care where it is... a warehouse, a living room, a school gym, a bar, a cathedral. Those are only the props. Please! Let's provide a place where people aren't consumers, customers, pawns, subscribers, supporters, adherents or disciples. Rather, let's provide a place where we can actually discover ourselves, and just be a person for a while... a place where we are not judged or cajoled, cataloged or categorized, lured or lead, envisioned or enabled, improved or empowered, managed or manipulated.

Is there any such place on earth?

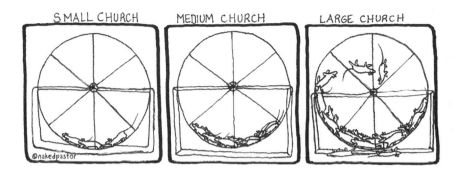

Stripped Bare (October 31, 2009)

Many people are tired of doing church in the same old way (point A). Some seem to appreciate the way we are doing church here (point B), and wonder how they can get from point A to point B.

First of all, I want to assert that if these people moved here and became a part of our church, they would in soon realize that there is nothing spectacular about it. There is nothing to boast and nothing to reproduce. Like I continually tell people, I spend most of my time deconstructing, preventing things from happening, and resisting success. I am constantly reprimanded for our church being self-sabotaging in that we continually seem to undermine strategies that might guarantee some measure of stability and even growth. Believe me, there are times we would love successful growth with its stability and all that it provides, but when we are at our best, we resist these temptations.

What I can say is that, as a church, we are pretty much stripped bare of goal, vision and agenda. We can say, for the most part, that we don't coerce, manipulate, or control people. People are free to come and go as they are and as they please. It is a completely voluntary assemblage with no expectations placed upon it. We do not prescribe beliefs or lifestyles. If people come with agendas or some people develop agendas, they don't seem to last. Their sense of what a church should be gets frustrated.

Lisa and I have been married for almost 30 years. We have a rich relationship. If other couples desiring a good relationship came to us to learn how, we could give some pointers. We could even allow them to observe us for a while. But I'm confident that in time they would start asking, *"What's the big deal?"* There are no tricks or formulas. It's mostly mundane commitment and tenacious hard work. It's the same with our church community. There's no magic, no flash, no tricks, no formulas, no big attraction. Our worship music is raw and unprofessional. The teaching is unrefined, crude and informal. Our community is made up of a diverse mixture of regular people. We aren't a big deal.

Therefore, even though you might want to deconstruct your church, it isn't pretty. But I think it is worthwhile and even necessary if you are to become more free and more human, and if you want to discover what true community and love is. So, I'm thinking I might blog for a while on how our church has deconstructed over the years. It is a wild and fascinating story, and many feel it is a story that needs to be told. So stay tuned!

The Omnivore's Dilemma and Spirituality (November 18, 2009)

I'm reading Michael Pollan's book, *The Omnivore's Dilemma: A Natural History of Four Meals*. I want to quote one sentence from his introduction:

> ... I wonder if it doesn't make more sense to speak in terms of an American paradox– that is, a notably unhealthy people obsessed by the idea of eating healthily.

When I read that, I was immediately reminded of something that has happened not infrequently in my personal life concerning spirituality. For so many years I had been seeking hard for some answers. Although I had been in the church since I was 16 years old and read and studied the Bible ever since; even though I had gone to bible college and seminary

and university to get my several degrees; even though I have been preaching and teaching in the church for all this time, I felt deep down that something was missing. I was thoroughly unsatisfied. The Christian culture I found myself in couldn't give me peace about how other religions fit into the scheme of things, or how people of other faiths or non-faiths were also on a valid path. I met with spiritual directors and masters from different traditions; I prayed, meditated, contemplated, read so many books from so many streams, wrote scores of journals, all in an attempt to find some understanding and peace. I was an intense spiritual seeker.

I drove my wife Lisa nuts! I remember her so many times saying to me that the more spiritual I got, the less attractive I became to her. The more peace I sought, the more agitated I became. The more understanding I sought, the more stupid I would behave. Bottom line: the more I sought, the more lost I became.

I finally realized something I knew all along: there's no way to reconcile all the complexity of ideas, faiths, traditions, philosophies, and spiritualities that are out there. I finally saw that all these things are ripples riding on the top of a deep current of a disguised unity. The apparent divisions were all unfolding of a deeper and mysterious Oneness. I apprehended the truth that I had to die to all my brain's attempts to grasp for knowledge. I had to humble myself, die to self, and, in a sense, give up the search. It was necessary for me to, in way, stop struggling to stay on the tumultuous surface and sink, sink way down. It is then and there that I found, almost by accident, what I had been looking for. And it is far more wonderful than I could imagine or explain.

10 Challenges of Religious Communities (December 20, 2009)

I speak from a Christian perspective here as it relates to the church. But these 10 points can also be applied to any denomination and even any religion. I am in solidarity with those who struggle to stay in the church, with those who have left it, as well as those who desire to be a part of a spiritual community but won't for various reasons. I consider these my mission field. These points below are only from my experience, and they all can be prefaced with "generally speaking". Just consider them:

1. I've experienced enough **abuse**, intrigue, exploitation and alienation within the church, and have heard enough first hand testimonies from others, to realize that it isn't rare within this institution.
2. My experience of church in the past tells me that I am to

believe what is expected and what I am told.

3. **Questions**, unless they complement the accepted tradition and dogma, are not welcomed.
4. I've found that **friendship** within the church is not based on love for the person, but on a conditional compatibility.
5. The church is notorious for supporting **codependency**. Refuse to play this game and you're considered cruel.
6. **Success** measured by money, numbers, appearance and reputation, is the gauge of choice. If you redefine what true success is and live by that, you're considered a failure.
7. **Creativity** has difficulty finding a home here. Unless it is religious art.
8. **Exclusion** trumps inclusion. Gays, for example! Diversity is scary and deemed impossible.
9. **Male** dominated. The fascination with power, authority, strategy, chain of command, visions and goals, reflect this.
10. The threatening demand to adhere to a **literalist** interpretation of scripture is always the axe waiting to fall and sever you from the group.

Open Round Table #3 (February 3, 2010)

We had another Open Round Table meeting for our church community again last night. Although we have a kind of body of executive elders to make crucial financial decisions, etc., about the church, we want the oversight of the church to be open and collegial. We don't have a membership role at Rothesay Vineyard. So anyone who is at all interested in the welfare of the church and wishes to have a voice in its health is welcome to come. Approximately 20 or so people attend. I would like to see more. But it is totally volunteer based. No pressure on anyone to attend or skip. Anyone can play or not.

This isn't just talk. We are serious about it. I opened the meeting by reading Psalm 133 where it talks about unity and harmony. How good and pleasant it is when brothers and sisters dwell together in unity. After some beautifully picturesque descriptions of what this unity looks like, it closes by saying that where this unity is kept, "there the Lord ordains his blessing". I feel it is our task to maintain harmony. God, in turn, will bless that. Unity and harmony is blessed. We have these meetings so that we can maintain harmony among ourselves. This is an exercise in unity. They can hear my heart, and I can hear theirs. Together we can hear the heart of God for the church and the heart of the church for God.

As usual I went into the meeting nervous because I don't carry an agenda with me. I try to empty my mind of all motive and desire so that we can have a true and open dialog. Together we will care for this community and through our conversation discover how to do this well. As usual there are awkward moments of silence at the beginning. But once a conversation starts, that hour and a half is a wonderfully chaotic exchange of energy and ideas. We don't reach any conclusions necessarily. We just get a feel for each other and the community. These are a few of the things that emerged in our conversation:

1. We are different and unique and hard to describe. But we like it and wouldn't trade it for anything else. What we don't need is a mission statement or a vision. What we might need is a language to describe ourselves. What we might need is what the Bible calls giving a reason for the hope that is within us. We believe that as we shine our own light with truth and integrity, that this will be the way we love those around us.

2. We are sitting on a huge asset of over 15 acres of prime commercial or industrial land. We also own a very functional building. However, we have developed in such a way that it doesn't really match our personality as a community right now. We are not sure what to do about it yet, but there was a lot of energy and discussion about what the possibilities are. I admired the sense of adventure the people shared, as well as their

courageous willingness to take risks to become more integrated in all that we are and do.

For the past couple of weeks I have been hearing lots of criticism and negative rumors about me as well as the church. I allowed them to get me down. I would enter very dark moments when I questioned my own call, the church, and even my own sanity. But when those who care about the community gathered together last night, all those phantom rumors evaporated in our mutual love for God, each other and the church. I left encouraged and fortified to fulfill my call.

Principalities and Powers as Created Beings (March 12, 2010)

All institutions belong to the category of principalities and powers. They are not inherently evil. The principalities and powers are, like all things, created. We are to have dominion over them, not them over us. They are to serve us. Not us them. This includes the institution we call the church.

A few weeks ago I attended what we might call a house church of young adults. I was asked to come and share with them some of my thoughts. We met in a living room. There was food and wine. It was fun. We had communion, had a theological discussion, and there was prayer. What was missing was this sense of expectation that an institution imposes on people. There was no overriding agenda that had to be met. These young people were free of the constant surveillance that the church often exercises over its members.

Their spiritual condition was their own personal responsibility, and they gathered occasionally to encourage one another. They didn't come hoping that this would fill a void in their own lives. We just gathered as friends. Even though there was the

"Lord, I thank you that I have such a peaceful church."

recognition of commitment and even love, I came free and left free. I realize that it is easier to achieve this without a building, staff, budgets and charters, etc. But it was refreshing.

This isn't easy to accomplish. It means constantly challenging the principalities and powers, the institution, to humble itself, relinquish its vision and agenda that is often dehumanizing, and serve us.

Serve Vision or People (March 15, 2010)

Vision is incompatible with church community. The vision and mission statement talk is very provocative and tempting. As soon as anyone questions what our purpose is, it has the immediate and alluring aura of imagining, creating and shaping our future. It's called "futuring". It is very sexy. If you are a business or an influence or lobby group or club or even a charity or anything else, you will need to have a vision and articulate a mission statement. But not a church. People, even believers, must have the freedom to assemble without being required to serve a vision created by the pastor or the leaders or even the collective. Otherwise their personal freedom out of necessity is sublimated. You have a choice: you either serve a vision or you serve people. The church can't do both.

Behind Enemy Lines (March 17, 2010)

I was telling a friend today that sometimes I feel like a voice crying in the wilderness. I sense I am working behind enemy lines in very hostile territory. My pastoral style is very different. I know that. Our church community is also very different. We know that. The result of my and our uniqueness brings harassment verbally, socially, spiritually, etc. Here are just some of the reasons:

1. You can believe however you want if you want. You do anyway.
2. You need not have to fear the constant surveillance of behavior.
3. You do not have to submit to, support, or subject yourself to a vision.
4. You are free to question. Even the pastor! Take that both ways.
5. You aren't pressured at all into giving your money.
6. You need not be ashamed of your failures or weaknesses, perceived or otherwise.
7. You aren't expected to fit into a certain lifestyle.
8. You can embrace and/or choose your own orientation.
9. You can bring your unedited authentic self into the community.
10. You do not have to fear authority, manipulation or control.

We don't look unique. But the spirit of the community is definitely unique. You'd have to be here to feel what I mean. You are welcome anytime!

Quarter of a Century (April 6, 2010)

I've finally left the professional ministry. I was ordained 25 years ago. I was a student minister before that. It has been a long hard haul. But I've gradually come to the realization that I can no longer work inside of that system. I no longer seem to fit within the institution. This is not to say that I don't believe in the church. I absolutely do. But my relationship to the organization has definitely changed. This blog has always been about my critique of the church. I believe in the right and the importance of Christians to gather. The same would apply to people of other faiths, beliefs, philosophies, etc. But it's the bad stuff that creeps in and clings to the gathering that I've always been critical of.

One of the most deadly influences on a community is agenda. In my opinion, it should be enough to gather together to study the bible, pray, worship and fellowship. It's when we desire more that things to go awry. To come without an agenda, without a goal, without a dream, without a vision for the church is extremely difficult. But this is the only way a church will live in a healthy manner. Visionary thinking, fantasizing, kills the church. Even the slightest bit of fantasizing for the church, like a little leaven, will affect the whole lump. It must be renounced entirely.

I plan on continuing this blog as a kind of virtual free-range pastor. I will continue my critique of all things spiritual and religious and institutional. Perhaps I will be even more liberated to express my thoughts. Thanks for all your kind and encouraging words.

Frustrate Visionary Thinking (April 20, 2010)

To impose a vision upon a church is not only unhealthy, but deadly to the genuine life of the church. I've seen it happen over and over again. Even a vision that is inspired by the community is a self-destructive force. What would it be like just to gather, worship, pray and teach the scripture, and love one another? To the modern mind, this isn't enough. The powerful prefer to see us not as human beings, but as commodities. They see this mass of people as a resource for a greater purpose. They are spiritual lobbyists who recognize the

usefulness of groups to effect change. They are businessmen. They are not pastors. They aren't interested in the flock of God, but in the utilization of corporate power.

Here are ways to frustrate visionary thinking in your church:

1. It is one thing for individuals to have personal visions and dreams. It is the application of these to a community that is dangerous.
2. Don't see the church group as an entity, but primarily a voluntary gathering of free individuals.
3. Similarly, the church as an entity cannot fix people's problems or make their lives happy. It is their own responsibility that other individuals can assist in.
4. Embrace diversity of thought and expression. Do not set goals for the church.
5. Do not measure success in terms of numbers, money or reputation.
6. See that mission is expressed individually. Each person is salt and light.

7. Any corporate mission that is genuine will seem spontaneous and have an "of course" feeling to it.
8. Share the oversight of the church. Avoid autocratic rule that provides the richest culture for visionary thinking.
9. Don't pretend to know the future of the church prophetically, statistically or otherwise. You don't!
10. Respect the pressure the people are under to want a king, to desire favor, and to think in terms of marketing to promote success. Almost all the literature available is written by successful pastors of successful churches. Don't bow to this pressure.

Biblical Arguments Against Vision (April 22, 2010)

1. The verse most often used to support vision in a church is Proverbs 29:18... *"Without a vision, the people perish."* But even an elementary study of that verse will reveal that the word translated *"vision"* is best translated *"prophecy"* or *"revelation"*. It isn't talking about the modern preoccupation with creating and articulating a vision over a group of people to maintain health or secure life or success. It's more related to the biblical theme, *"We do not live by bread alone, but by every word that proceeds from the mouth of God."* Without revelation, without the truth coming to us, we would die.
2. There is no talk about vision for each local church in the New Testament. I suggest the earliest church's concern is primarily a human one: the urgent necessity of fellowship, the gathering together of those with the same belief in a hostile environment. Then it is out of this that worship, prayer and apostolic teaching find expression. Not even evangelism is its primary concern. The New Testament assumes evangelism is the byproduct of the presence of the church in society. For instance, in Acts, the earliest Christians didn't disperse in order to evangelize. Instead, the church dispersed after each increase in persecution, and people were added to the

church as a result. Which of course brings to mind that this obsession with vision is a modern one. From the earliest church to the post-modern era, it wasn't a concern. Now, it seems to me, vision is a modern technique for attracting, keeping and motivating people in the midst of heated competition.

3. Philippians 2: 5 encourages the members of the church to be like-minded. This doesn't mean theologically or ideologically. For Paul instantaneously launches into one of the earliest hymns of the church concerning the humiliation of Christ. For Paul, like-mindedness isn't agreement, but humility. In fact, later in Philippians 3: 15, Paul intimates diversity of thought. To seek unanimity on a vision statement is unfair to some of the members at least.

4. To articulate a vision and align a church under it assumes we can predict and shape our future by our present thoughts and actions. It falls into the old cause and effect trap: do this and that will happen. In other words, it removes God and the need for God as Lord. Even with the most fervent prayer and discernment, the vision requires God to undersign our agenda, no matter how noble or spiritual it might seem. To conjure up a vision for our actions in order to determine our future is in my mind paramount to visiting the witch of Endor (1 Samuel 28).

5. Jesus' own *modus operandi* was, "*My food is to do the will of him who sent me...*" (John 4: 34). I suggest that just as the scriptures teach that God provides for and feeds his people daily (manna and daily bread), Jesus was fed daily with the will of God. The overarching themes of coming to seek and to save and to serve found daily and spontaneous expressions in the life of Jesus.

6. The story of Simon the Sorcerer applies here (Acts 8). The disciples were doing something for others freely and spontaneously, motivated by love and inclusion. But

Simon wanted to package it into a predictable program with guaranteed success. In the same way, to turn God's will (example: seek, save and serve) into a vision statement mutates the biblical order of command and obedience into the worldly order of goal and achievement).

7. Psalm 139: 16 states that, *"All the days ordained for me were written in your book before one of them came to be."* A vision statement discerned by the church, articulated by the leader and administered by the leadership subtly transfers the power of our unknown yet preordained future from God's hands into human hands. With a slight and subtle shift, we organize under the words of authorities.

8. The biblical narrative favors diversity and dispersion. In the Garden, the vast variety of creatures are distinguished and separated by names. Babel attempts to gather everyone under one vision and they are scattered. Egypt attempts to gather all God's people under one mission and they are delivered. Israel attempts to reinforce its security but is dispersed into exile. The earliest church would have preferred to stay in the original hometown of Jerusalem but is persecuted and dispersed. Paul's greatest adversity was the attempt by Jerusalem to attain and maintain sovereignty over all believers. The Antichrist would sublimate all people under his power and authority but will be destroyed in the end. Organized gathering in the bible usually ends up as slavery or domination. I am surprised that often those most vehemently arguing in favor of vision (a unifying power over a group of people) are also the same ones who believe in the Antichrist, who's obvious purpose is to deceive even the elect and sublimate everyone under his charisma… because his vision will be plausible and spiritual.

9. Psalm 1: 1 says, *"Blessed is the man who does not walk in the counsel of the wicked…"*. The later translations, in

an attempt to neutralize the text, has translated it, *"Happy are those..."* which compromises the whole point of that Psalm, which articulates the biblical importance of the righteous individual. The fact that it is the first psalm is not an accident, for it launches the whole Psalter in the direction of individual faith that composes the community of faith. Although the bible obviously teaches the assembly of the righteous, it doesn't consider it a controlled clump, but a gathering of righteous ones, those who have *"worked out their own salvation with fear and trembling"* (Philippians 2:12).

10. The principalities and powers find expression in organizations and institutions, including the church. I suggest that the church is simply a voluntary gathering of individuals, and it is healthiest to keep them free of an all-encompassing vision that is an attempt to collect all the members under one power. To captivate people *"through philosophy and empty deceit, according to human tradition, according to the elemental spirits of the universe"* (Colossians 2: 8), is a benevolent dictatorship, but still a dictatorship. And this is why it is so deliciously deceptive: vision statements are usually plausible, they sound biblical, they are inspirational, and they hold out the hope that all these people can be controlled under one motivating idea, which in the end is demonic.

Cartoon: Lord of the Things (April 26, 2010)

Vision is okay in some contexts. And then only sometimes. But not in the church. I'm becoming more and more convinced that it is a corrosive power the church needs protection against. Even Jason Fried and David Heinemeier Hansson in the great book ReWork say, *"Unless you're a fortune-teller, long-term business planning is a fantasy."*

One thing to rule them all;
One thing to find them;
One thing to bring them all,
And in the darkness bind them.

©nakedpastor

Vision and Dis-ease (April 29, 2010)

You like your church. You've found a community that seems healthy to you. You've been there for over a year now. You feel the freedom to find your own spiritual path and to walk it with integrity without fear of judgment. The teaching is good. The conversational approach to the teaching time encourages you to seek and to find with curiosity and courage. It challenges you to think for yourself. The pastor takes a hands-off approach that you find refreshing, respectful and liberating. You know if

129

you have any questions, they will be respected and that resources will be made available to you to assist you in your individual search if you want. The worship is great too. The band is usually awesome and you like the music. The people feel free to experience it wholeheartedly if they want to. Your kids enjoy it. There are groups for them to join if desired. You have friends in this community. You feel connected. You know that if hard times come, there will be people to pray for you and support you in any way they can. You are given the opportunity to give, knowing that the church will not only use the money to support its own ministry, but also because you know the church is generous with its money in helping other churches and people in need. You are a part of this church because it augments your spiritual life in an integrative, holistic way, and doesn't violate your freedoms, person and values. Even though you commit yourself to the community, you still feel you are an authentically free individual and are respected as such. You don't feel sucked into some kind of religious vortex where you lose your voice and freedom and path, and you appreciate that. You have found a family and a home that has special meaning in your life.

Then one Sunday, the pastor says that he senses that something's missing. You are perplexed. What could be missing? This church already seems healthy to you. He goes on to say that he's decided the church needs a vision. He informs the congregation that he and the elders are going to start praying for a vision and start working on a mission statement.

You are disappointed. It saddens you that something so beautiful has suddenly been poisoned with expressions of discontent, ambition, and the destructive desire for the illusive "more" that you've learned to recognize.

You've seen this before in the last church you attended where they wanted more people and cloaked it in the language of evangelism.

And the church before that which wanted more money and cloaked it in the language of spiritual prosperity and charity.

And the church before that which wanted more programs and people to run them and cloaked it in the language of seeker-sensitivity.

And the church before that which wanted more of the Spirit to show up during worship and cloaked it in the language of renewal and spiritual passion.

You are getting tired. Can any community simply gather and just be happy to do the basics with peace, tranquility, joy and contentment? You wonder if any community can be free of this dis-ease.

Weed and Wolf (May 17, 2010)

What is most dangerous to the church? What is the most wicked weed and the most wily wolf? What weed looks delicious but is a terrible poison? What wolf wears the most convincing sheep costume to worm its way into the flock, its very food?

Over the many years I have been in the ministry, this is what I've concluded is most dangerous: Not sin. Not poverty. Not corruption. Not persecution. Not bad pastors. Not even poor theology. We will have these with us always. The greatest danger to the church is vision. Agenda. It is an idea for the church that certain people entertain that is the greatest danger to it. It is when different people have designs for the church, where they want it to be something other than what it is, that it destroys the fabric of the community. Even the most well-meaning people, believing that they want what's best for the church, in actuality introduce what is worst for it.

I have been on both sides: I've allowed my ideas for the church to bring damage to it, and seen other people's ideas do the same. This is the worst weeds and the worst wolves to the flock. This is what can slowly poison the community and bring sudden destruction to the fellowship, jeopardizing the actual life of what we think we are most concerned about. In desiring it to be more or different than what it is, we sabotage the beauty of what it actually already is. And this is what kills it.

A List on Building Community (July 19, 2010)

I had an interesting and enjoyable conversation with a young man today. He wanted to talk with me about building a community based church. He said that there are all kinds of materials out there on traditional models of doing church. But there is hardly anything out there concerned with building a church that emphasizes relationship and community. Almost all material out there is on how to tweak style, not substance. He asked me if I knew of any. No. Not much. He said that he's saved a file of all my posts on community. He wanted to talk with me about it. So he called me and we had a good chat.

Here are some of the things we talked about:

1. There are no **rules** to follow. If few are doing it, then they are doing it in their own unique contexts with their own unique people in their own unique way. There aren't grand general rules that apply to all situations.
2. It's like being a pioneer or an **explorer**. I have a good friend who teases me about comparing what I did as a pastor to being an explorer. I admit: my physical life is not in danger. I'm not living on seal blubber and sucking on snow in sub-zero temperatures. The dangers I faced are different. But they are just as real. It is no joke pioneering this kind of church community. It is serious business. And it takes a great deal of courage. But if you value it, it's worth it. What materials are out there on doing what he wants to do? Hardly anything. Are there materials out there on how to be a pioneer? What does that take? Guts. Resilience. Period.

3.   I compare what I was trying to do with being a **family**. My family would rebel if I tried to be their autocratic, charismatic, visionary leader. Businesses and countries are a whole other matter. If you want to build a corporation, then be that kind of leader. If you want to build community and be a part of it yourself, treat it like family.

4.   **Flexibility**. You have to do it one day at a time. Although you might have some general values that you embrace, strategizing weeks or months or years ahead is a futile exercise. It's like your family: you have values. You can generally plan ahead. But if you have kids, you know that each day is a new day and must be executed freshly.

5.   Be openly **humble**. Admit to your people that you don't really know what you're doing or how this is going to turn out. You are learning one day at a time. You are learning and discovering together. You are not the all-knowing leader.

6.   He was concerned about **burn-out**. Lisa and I found it interesting that we couldn't tell if we were always working or if we were just always hanging out with our friends. That's what community is. I rarely met people in my study. I always avoided the feeling of clinical. That's not family. Rather, we always met over coffee, lunch, or wine in the evenings. And Lisa and I made it a point of taking an evening or two to ourselves and a day on the weekend. Easy-peasy.

7.   **Smaller groups** help glue the community. Each smaller part strengthens the larger part. This is where everyone gets to play, experiment and experience community up close and personal. However… and this is something else I've discovered over the years… a smaller group with disgruntled members can cause problems.

8.   **Chaos theory**: it is messy, unpredictable and unattractive. When people discover a place where they can experiment in authenticity and encounter the authenticity of the other, sparks fly. Some start fires that

destroy. But some start fires that warm the heart. People won't flock to it for it's appeal. But those who want to experience community will trickle in.

9. This kind of community can attract very **needy** people. Some stay and find healing. Some stay until they figure their needs aren't being met according to their liking and leave. This can include the pastor.

10. My experience is that **money** can be a problem with this kind of community. If you want community, it takes volunteerism. Which means you can't employ the tithing campaign. You will rely on people's goodwill. Which sometimes runs thin. But those who believe in what you are doing and value such a community will bless it beyond their means.

This is just a start but I ended at 10. I like lists of 10.

Wanted: Dead and Alive! (August 10, 2010)

The most mature spiritual person can actually seem to be the most childlike. There is a confusing enigmatic character to the spiritual life in general.

But when you gather different spiritual lives in one community, the anomaly compounds exponentially. Community life **should** feel paradoxical. Especially the religious community life. The healthiest churches might actually appear to be the least healthy.

This is because **diversity** is more valuable as a sign of health than homogeneity. In my experience, homogeneity is usually forced and should always be held suspect. Homogeneity, again in my experience, has always been a thin veneer of conformity necessitated by the powers.

Paradox is not easy to live with. The mind is uncomfortable with it and wants to settle on one or the other of the opposing ideas. But as one matures and develops the art of holding two apparently opposing ideas simultaneously in the mind, paradox is understood at a very deep level. Then one can see life at work where death seems to prevail. And one can also see death at work where there proposes to be life. Or, as in a church, one can perceive a deep order in the midst of chaos. And one can perceive deep division where the primary presentation is homogeneity.

I saw love in our chaotic community, and that was its order. Love is the bonding agent manifesting the unity of the Spirit. It

is not agreement. It is not compatibility. It is not adherence, obedience, charismata, style or anything else. It is love that manifests itself in voluntary and willing fellowship with others who are different, even on significant levels.

Which is why it is difficult to keep a church together that is paradoxical in nature. Different people, from the pastor to the visitor, are always pressuring, lobbying, praying, expecting, longing and working for their own fantasies of what the church should be to become a reality.

We must rest in the paradoxical truth that the church can seem **alive** and **dead** at the same time.

Vision: I Cast You Out! (August 26, 2010)

I come back to the issue of vision and mission statements again and again because it is very important to me. It is also extremely important to the church. I have witnessed and experienced this first hand. This is not theoretical, but practical help for churches. I have seen and experienced the negative impact vision and mission statements have upon the church, and I wish churches would stop needing them, creating them, drafting them and casting them. The church would be healthier for it.

So here are just 10 reasons why vision and mission statements should be expelled from the life of the church.

Vision and mission statements…

1. **distract** from the primary purpose of the church, which is to *be* a community… a spiritual family, and focus attention and energy on *doing* something. I've seen meetings where critical relational issues were ignored in order to prioritize a vision's immediate demands.
2. **tantalize** the people to follow a code rather than their own hearts. How many times have I heard it said, when a unique need presented itself to the community, *"Well, that's not what we do!"*
3. **aren't found** from the earliest church right through to recent history. They are a modern phenomenon excited by their success in the business world. I believe they are necessary in business, but are a virus to the church. Inject just a small dose and in time it will crash the vitality of the local spiritual family. They might produce more activity, even positive activity, but the core health of the spiritual family will be compromised.
4. **promise** the success and longevity of the group rather than the individual health of its members.
5. **transfigure** what is meant to be a spiritual family into an energy unit, a lobby group, or an activist organization.

There is nothing wrong with these things, as long as we understand that this is a forsaking of our primary identity as a family. It would be like Lisa and I insisting that we were put on this earth to raise 3 children, when in fact our primary identity and role is lovers from which child-rearing emanates.

6. **insinuate** competition between local churches. Whenever I've been in meetings where demands for vision and mission statements were given, it always threw me back to Israel demanding a king because all of her enemies did. God consented. We are allowed to create and employ vision and mission statements without God smiting us. But that doesn't mean its the best way.

7. **divert** the pastor's attention away from the primary practice of prayer, study of scripture and teaching. Rather, the pastor's attention and energy usually get poured into inventing and crafting a sexy vision statement, convincing the leaders to endorse it, and inducing the congregation to comply to it.

8. **assume** we can predict the future and predetermine our actions in it. Almost all people I've spoken with admit that the vision and mission statement of their community is quickly redesigned, abandoned or forgotten as soon as tomorrow hits with full force.

9. **behave** like an addictive drug: once you buy in, you can never find the perfect high. They constantly lose their appeal and demand that they be traded up into something stronger and more satisfying.

10. **tempt** us to take our attention away from *what is right now* to *what should be by now*. They introduce a subtle dissatisfaction with who and what is, and instill an appetite for something better than what we already have right here right now.

Online & Local Community Similarities (September 21, 2010)

Many religious leaders bemoan the fact that some people are trying to find community online rather than locally. They feel that this is false, superficial and actually depreciates real community with a geographic location. They feel that such a person doesn't understand, value or benefit from a physical community.

I've come to the conclusion that online communities are very much the same as local communities. What I mean to say is that in many ways my "church" at nakedpastor behaves the same way as my local congregation did. It's almost uncanny!

So, whether we are willing to admit it or not, here are just some of the similarities:

1. People will be just as committed to the online community in terms of **involvement** as they are locally. People vote with their feet (and their money, but that's for later). People can't be forced to stay.
2. People will **give** money only when they feel like it. Required tithing in a local congregation is matched by subscription or membership fees online, or continual pressure to give online.
3. People will **help** others in the community when they feel like it. I've seen all kinds of different kinds of help passing hands online at nakedpastor... things like a listening ear, encouragement, prayer, money, gifts, and just plain old time.
4. People will change the **quality** of the community for good or bad. In other words, some people will enhance the community with love, care and kindness, and some will challenge the community by being belligerent, nasty and even abusive to others. They use their anonymity as a cover for their cruelty.
5. People will bring their own theological or ideological **mindsets** to the community and are naturally very resistant to change. They will change their minds on their own terms. Acquiescence often conceals doubt or even

disagreement in order to conform and continue in the community.

6. People will form tighter relationships and even **friendships** within the online community, just like locally. Some might even have affairs with one another. Maybe the blogger will run off with one of his members.

7. People will **express** their own opinions and contribute to the development of the community if given a chance. In fact, online communities are excellent for this kind of community. However, as with the local scene, online communities will for the most part attract similar readers and members, unless the moderator endeavors to provide a context for diversity of opinion, thought, belief and expression.

8. People will, if they desire it, develop a personal and working **relationship** with the blogger to the extent they are allowed. Having online pastors, spiritual directors, priests, ministers, Imams, Rabbis, gurus, etc., can be a positive thing.

9. People will, for the most part, respond **negatively** to feeling victimized by the website's moderator and the community. If they feel they are being pressured into adopting the writer's point of view or to embrace their vision without their own approval, they will leave freely, as they should

10. People will, for the most part, respond **positively** to wise oversight and diligent moderation of the community.

Pastor Be Yourself! (October 18, 2010)

One of the greatest challenges for me as a pastor is to not succumb to the constant pressure of expectation. Members have fantasies of what their pastor should be. Church organizations, denominations or movements have fantasies of what its pastors should be. But worst of all, pastors themselves have fantasies of what they should be or would like to be.

I make it my personal challenge to be exactly who I am: myself. I also encourage others to be exactly who they are.

I often took great comfort from something Karl Barth wrote in his fine little book, *Homiletics*:

> *It is as the persons they are that preachers are called to this task, as these specific people with their own characteristics and histories. It is as the persons they are that they have been selected and called. This is what is meant by originality. Pastors are not to adopt a role. They are not to slip into the clothing of biblical characters. That would be the worst kind of comedy. They are not to be Luthers, churchmen, prophets, visionaries, or the like. They are simply to be themselves, and to expound the text as such. Preaching is the responsible word of a person of our own time. Having heard myself, I am called upon to pass on what I have heard. Even as ministers, it matters that these persons be what they are. They must not put on a character or a robe. They do not have to play a role. It is you who have been commissioned, you, just as you are, not as minister, as pastor or theologian, not under any concealment or cover, but you yourself have simply to discharge this commission.*

I would encourage pastors everywhere to find the courage to live up to this arduous but simple task. I realize and personally know the cost of taking such a risk. You might risk losing support, popularity, your church and even your job. But would you rather lose that or yourself?

I made an image of Karl Barth based on the last photograph taken of him, smoking his pipe in his study.

Whistle-Blowers Club (October 23, 2010)

All systems cultivate fear and encourage silence among its members. This cannot be found in their vision statements or goals or charters. Even though systems or organizations mean well, this cultivation of fear and the encouragement of silence predominates the system's relationship with its members. It is

not intentional or calculated. When it comes to that you have something like fascism.

It is very difficult to expose the problems in a system. It is considered betrayal. And to betray a system results in bad repercussions... even losing your job. You will pay a serious price for challenging, questioning or blowing the whistle on the system you are a member of. This is why it is so difficult to get whistle-blowers. It might cost them their lives... financially or maybe even physically.

I was talking with a friend a few weeks ago who expressed his frustration at the system he worked within. He had a problem with HR's decision. He knew that if he challenged HR's decision there would be negative repercussions. He would be blackballed, his check would get stalled in the system, and he might even lose his job.

I knew exactly what he was talking about because I experienced the same kind of dynamic in churches. I may

have loved my work, but if (or should I say "when"?) I questioned the system it was considered paramount to biting the hand that fed me. You just don't get away with that for very long.

Systems can't be helped. They will always be with us. Even if whistle-blowers started a club, to blow the whistle on that club would incur the same repercussions.

Unrelenting Pressure (October 28, 2010)

In an age when we are constantly bombarded with advertising, vision statements, and goal-oriented living, wouldn't it be nice to find maybe one or two hours a week when you could gather together with other people without these pressures?

I think so.

One thing I do as a pastor is allow space that is totally free of these constant unrelenting pressures. Even such noble pressures as spiritual ones are just as deadly, if not deadlier. I would meditate on grace and love, believing that the power of these two very real realities would do any of the work that needed to be done.

Not everyone believes this. Most people believe that we need to be driving, pushing, pulling and prodding ourselves for the kingdom in order to improve ourselves and this world. Most people believe they need to make themselves and others worthy of this grace, and that once it is received they need to live worthily of it. Grace has only become the new law. Which isn't really grace.

Churches seem to be the most frenetic, hyperactive, and taut places around. Even though many people would say that we are a Sabbath people and that God does the work, most don't really believe it.

Insidious (December 4, 2010)

Is it possible for people to just gather as a community without investing the community with its own self-image? Is it possible for a community to be completely free of vision?

I'm not sure. I tried. I had to quit the last community I oversaw when I realized the tide had turned against this.

Some people might argue that my idea for a community to have no vision is in itself a vision. I disagree. Lincoln infuriated his critics by saying things like, "My policy is to have no policy." One could argue that his idea was a policy. But his point was that he really didn't have a policy. So when I say a church is healthiest without vision, I mean it purely and simply.

I issue a warning: As soon as a community forms and formulates an ideal of itself, this ideal takes on a personality that demands to be nourished and sustained. It will eventually require a global sovereignty over the members of that community. Even if it is a humble and noble ideal, it will enforce the same demands.

The result is that the formulated ideal of community becomes the reference through which relationship is conducted. The direct authenticity of relationship between the members is compromised. The community has become artificial.

I think many people have become wise to this, perhaps without knowing it. They are now suspicious of any religious community because of the rampant insidiousness of vision in communities they have experienced.

Church as Pointless (December 8, 2010)

I have always argued that churches are best to not be goal-oriented, that they should be free of vision. In my opinion, this is the healthiest church.

If a church has vision and is goal-oriented, then it has deviated from its healthiest self and will impose burdens on its members. It will have become something else... like a lobbying group, an activist group, a missional group, or something other than just a church. It can still call itself a church. But it should admit it has opted for a utilitarian identity rather than just accepting its identity. A church will have to choose to be utilitarian or just be. It can't be both.

In other words, churches should be pointless*. Pointless like my family is pointless. My family is not without its problems and issues, but it is a vibrant, rich, joyful and dynamic community. But it is completely pointless. It doesn't mean things don't happen or that we haven't had an affect on others or the world. But we are pointless. We're not even intentionally pointless. We are just pointless. And I love it for that. That's why I love to go home every day and just be, just relax, just love and be loved.

When I pastored local churches, I pastored them with the same thing in mind: that it should be pointless.

Very few people agree. I'm not sure why. Perhaps we are all caught up in the modern "vision" mindset and lingo. Perhaps most people never experienced or enjoyed just being in a loving family. Perhaps most people are ambitious and competitive and want to see their church advance beyond the others.

In any case, I've learned that most people and churches are uncomfortable with being pointless. I'll be writing more about this, so stay tuned.

*I am indebted to Terry Eagleton for the use of this word "*pointless*", although he uses it in reference to life in his wonderful little book, *The Meaning of Life*.

Church as Pointless #2 (December 9, 2010)

I've never understood why, when I say that a church should have no vision, some people leap to the conclusion that this means, as someone once said to me, that *"You just sit by the phone all day waiting for God to call."* Why do people assume that if you "be" that this excludes "do"?

Have they ever read about John the Baptist, our Old Testament hero spilling into the New, who lived in the austere desert his entire life shouting insanities?

Have they never heard of the entire Christian monastic movement, beginning with Anthony of Egypt in the third century, who prayed, consumed only bread and water, and weaved baskets?

Have they ever read, without a critical Christian eye, *Beginner's Mind*, a splendid Zen Buddhist text?

These all would emphasize "being". But I would also suggest

that they represent catalysts for significant change.

The Pastor's Dream

©nakedpastor

My family, as I said, is pointless. I said yesterday that this means that we don't serve a purpose. We are beyond the utilitarian agenda of the world around us. We delight in just being a family. As soon as any authority demands that my family be useful, we have tyranny.

Churches would be (or do) best to delight in just being. Does this mean that they will not be catalysts for change?

Maybe not. But also maybe!

A Letter From the Bride to Friends of the Bridegroom (December 28, 2010)

This is an idea I've been working on… a letter from the church to those who manage it. What do you think?

To Friends of the Bridegroom:

I am so very tired. You say you are friends of my Beloved. So why do you work me so hard? Why do you have so many expectations and place so many demands on me? You complain about my spots. But they are calluses formed by your industry. You complain about my wrinkles. But they are symptoms of the fatigue you have induced. I never sleep because you won't let me rest. I never rest because you won't let me stop. I am beleaguered by your ambitions.

You have so much vision for who I should be that you no longer know me. I am a complete stranger to you. I was beautiful once. He saw me. He pursued me. He courted me. He betrothed me. But you have forgotten this and have forgotten me. You do not respect me. So I fear you do not respect him either. You are repulsed by me. Yes I am plain. But I am lovely. Yes I am unadorned. But I am ravishing. But your eyes are so filled with ideas and ideals, visuals and visions, goods and goals. You no longer see me. You don't know me. I am fading from the earth and you are replacing me with a hideous imitation, a compilation of all your fantasies.

I am generous, kind and compassionate. But no one sees this anymore because of all the silly games and agonizing agendas you relentlessly push me into. If you would leave me be and let me be, perhaps you would rediscover my beauty, my allure, and my generosity to all who approach me and to all to whom I draw near. Oh how I would love to embrace so many friends in my arms. But they are tied with your intentions.

I am beautiful. I am wise. I am humble. I am compassionate. I am waiting. You don't love me.

I have been betrayed by the friends of my Beloved.

no longer yours,

The Bride

Choice: Family or Vision (January 3, 2011)

Do you want your church to be a family?

Or do you want your church to be a purpose group?

If you want it to be the first one, then you cannot have a vision or a goal. If you want to be the second one, then you'll need a vision and a goal.

You can't be both. Not at the same time.

As soon as you introduce vision and goal to a community, it cannot be a family. The healthy family is a place free of agenda, visions and goals. It is, as I've said before, pointless. It doesn't serve a purpose or fulfill an agenda. Once it does, it is no longer a free family, but a power unit wielded by the visionary.

This is not to denigrate the purpose group or church. However, we need to be clear that even though this purpose group may only experience family-like moments, it will not and cannot be a family-like community. This is also not to say that a family-like community cannot achieve things. But the things they do accomplish will be spontaneous, situational and maybe even uncontrollable.

You have to make a choice.

Cartoon: circus (January 4, 2011)

Recently I was talking with a pastor. (I talk with many so don't think it was you.) He was obviously burning out. He originally used to disagree with my thoughts about vision, but now he was beginning to see what I was getting at and he was sick of it. He realized it was useless to tweak the vision. They'd been doing that for years to no avail. He finally knew the whole thing had to be rejected altogether. But no one agreed with him. Of course! I wonder what will happen.

When he was telling me all he was doing, this cartoon is what I pictured.

Yes, this is how my mind works. It sees pictures before words or ideas.

Sorry. I draws 'em as I sees 'em.

Cartoon: The Vision Burden (January 5, 2011)

Jesus chastised religious leaders for laying heavy burdens on the backs of people and not lifting a finger to help them. Yet we don't blink an eye when we place the burden of vision on others. Just because it's cool. It's such a fad.

Businesses have vision and they pay people to fulfill it. Purpose groups have vision and they get people to commit to it. Focus groups have vision and they subscribe people to lobby it. The church isn't a business. It isn't a purpose group. It isn't a lobby group.

It may be one of these things necessarily and occasionally. But not primarily.

How to be Visionless (January 5, 2011)

Concerning the lack of vision, this is how it worked for me:

When I pastored my last local congregation, we didn't have a vision statement. Not until the end of my ministry there was there any talk of vision. We had no vision statement meetings, goal setting or vision-casting meetings or anything of the sort. We did talk about values. I resisted for as long as possible the whole vision industry.

We would explore things like grace, generosity and

compassion, and things like forgiveness and our solidarity with the whole human race. Things like that. I was confident, and still am, that if you care for the roots then along come the fruits. Provide pasture and protection and the sheep will prosper.

I was right. I was amazed, but not surprised, at the remarkable instances of generosity that I witnessed. The acts of kindness were sweet. Forgiveness, patience and compassion popped up unexpectedly and spontaneously. Remarkable acts of sacrifice would suddenly be performed. Most of the things took place through individuals, quietly, humbly, neighborly. Or there would be an inspiration from someone or a small group to do something. They planned it, did it, ended it and moved on. Sometimes a group would last long enough to complete a project. Sometimes it would last longer. Sometimes it would flop. No lights or horns.

In this way the church performed like a person not coerced but free… just like its members.

How a church does this is very important. But that's another post.

Crowd Control Starts With You (January 15, 2011)

I read this today on a Linkedin feed and I nearly spewed my coffee:

> *Church goals must be continually repeated and reinforced. Once isn't enough. People forget. To outperform you must overinform.*

I have questions:

1. Who ever said the church needs "*goals*"? Seriously!? The church has adopted business language and has swallowed it hook line and sinker. The fisherman's intentions are not good.
2. Is "*must*" high on your list of personal motivators?

3. When your church uses words like "*repeat*", does the word "*brainwash*" ever come to mind, if you have one?

4. Are your own inclinations so wayward and wrong that you continually have to hear an opposing message repeated over and over again to get you back on the church's track? Maybe you are like a beagle who can't help but perpetually run after new scents and must be leashed, caged or kennelled.

5. If your church says that they are going to "*reinforce*" an idea over and over again, repetitiously, does this not conjure up images of the Nazi youth, another very visionary religious movement?

6. If your church has to tell you something over and over again because "*once isn't enough*" because "*you will forget*", do you hear it implicitly saying, "*Because you're stupid*"?

7. Why will you "*forget*"? Have you ever in your life forgotten something that is centrally important to you?

8. If you are a part of a church who's agenda is to "*outperform*", who are you competing against? Other churches? Shame on you! Yourself? If it is yourself that you are outperforming, what's wrong with yourself right now that it needs to be outperformed? Who are you giving permission to continually tell you that you need to outperform yourself? Do you hate yourself that much?

9. Doesn't the bible have something to say about our obsession with competition and performance?

10. If any organization tells you upon joining that you will be overinformed, will you still sign up? Are you going to willingly subject yourself to overinformation, endless repetition, perpetual reinforcement and the constant call to outperform? Are you willingly going to subject yourself to the constant reminder that you're forgetful?

Yes, I have intentionally neglected the *purpose* of the church goals. Why? Because no matter how noble the goals, the means to achieving them are inhumane! Or maybe you believe the end does justify the means?

This is the kind of visionary thinking I abhor.

Only the Beleaguered Understand (January 17, 2011)

I would like to share with you an incident that may illustrate why I am so against vision and the driving of vision in the church:

This was years ago. I was out of the ministry at the time. I had been dismissed as an employee of an international ministry and as the pastor of the church that this ministry hired me to plant and grow. It was largely due to my style of pastoring that my boss and so many people still do not understand. It was a horrible time for me and my family. Fortunately, our previous church took us in and allowed us to hang out with them and recover from our rather serious wounds.

During this time I was urged to attend a workshop for burned-out pastors. Reluctantly, Lisa and I went. The room was full of pain. The leader of the workshop was basically teaching that we all needed to get away on a sabbatical and rest so that we could get back to what we were doing before only with more vision and vigor.

I lost it. I mean I *really* lost it… to the point where I embarrassed myself by my outburst. But I still meant it. My embarrassment was only augmented by the response of the group. They looked at me with pity. They took my impassioned response as proof of my burnout.

However, later in the day outside the workshop, a few people who were there came up to me secretly and in whispering tones admitted they knew exactly what I was talking about. They wondered if my idea of ministry and church community life was even remotely possible.

It was then that I realized that I could preach my lungs out about this, but that nobody but the completely beleaguered will understand what I am saying.

It is proved to this day. I get emails every week from pastors who are beyond the point of burn-out, completely wasted and ready to give up on the whole enterprise. And people who are tired of being pushed, disrespected, manipulated and coerced, but still want to be a part of a religious community.

Only these seem to understand.

Authority & Totalitarian Ideology (January 19, 2011)

As the philosopher Slavoj Žižek suggests, there is on the *"mere authoritarian lust for power"*, but there is also a *"totalitarian ideology"*.*

We would be best to resist the manifestation of these in the church.

It would not be in the church's or the member's best interest to allow the lust for power to be expressed in the church. Not only could we say it is it contrary to the spirit of Jesus, but contrary to what is best for people or the institutions they populate. But I have seen very little that discourages this authoritarian lust for power and very little to correct it when it is expressed. In fact, when we do see it, we call it "*strong*" or "*charismatic*" or "*focused*" leadership.

We would also be wise, in my opinion, not to allow totalitarian ideology to find its way into church life. However, it has found full acceptance. Žižek describes totalitarian ideology as *"the will to impose on reality a theoretically developed vision of a better world"*. In other words, we endorse and fund authoritarian pastors and their leaders to theoretically envision a better and even perfect church in their minds and to impose this vision upon the church-as-it-is, the people under their care. Even with mutual consent with the people, we must agree that this is disastrous.

Is it possible for the church to be released from these two related scourges?

(Living in the End Times)

Watch a Woman Undress (January 20, 2011)

I know I post about vision in the church a great deal. It is one of my pet peeves because I think it is probably the worst affliction the church suffers from.

My posts make some people angry, frustrated, or confused. I receive frequent comments or emails from people saying that my insistence that there should be no vision is, in itself, a vision. Others assert that my repetitive rant that it is unhealthy to envision change for the church and not respect what it presently is, is in itself to ask the church to change and to not appreciate it as it is.

I disagree. I still offer that vision is damaging to healthy church community life, and I also suggest that we are to love the church as it is, which implies not demanding that it change.

I came up with an analogy today that might help:

Have you ever watched a woman undress? (I use "woman" instead of "man" because, well, it's me writing. You can use whichever.) The woman is undressing. She is taking off her clothes. All of them! Maybe she's going to take a bath or sleep nude or streak or whatever. Would you say that she is changing? No. Of course not! She is undressing, stripping to her essential self. Neither is this vision or fantasy, because I do not imagine her as different than she actually is as her naked self standing before me. I might fantasize what to do with her now, but that's another discussion.

This is what I argue about. I see things like vision and purpose-drivenness as accretions that are not only unnecessary, but hindrances to church community life that can be stripped away

157

easily, quickly and beneficially.

Beautifully Unaware (January 21, 2011)

I'm editing my new upcoming book on *Vision*. It will include cartoons. I'm quite excited about it.

I went back through my blog gleaning all relevant posts. So last night I took a sort of fly-over of the whole history of my blog. I made an interesting discovery from my years of pastoring my last church:

We were at our best when we were at our worst.

In other words, when we were struggling with something: cancer, accident, the death of a loved one through cancer, suicide or heart attack or something else, financial disaster, personal bankruptcy, ridicule from other churches, gay rights and full inclusion, pregnancy before marriage, miscarriages, etc., etc., etc...

I read the notes I've kept from people during these times expressing how grateful they were for the church in all its simplicity and weakness, authenticity and genuineness, its raw and unpretentious nature that allowed them to be themselves, to find healing, and to be restored to contributing compassionate citizens of this world.

Adversely, it was when everything was going smoothly that trouble started stirring. It was during the doldrums when people got restless, impatient, ambitious, and, for lack of a better word, grouchy.

When our focus changed from compassionately caring for someone in our midst in deep anguish, pain and sorrow to wanting to become something... that was when we got ugly. In my opinion.

The Cross and Deconstruction (January 23, 2011)

In Christian theology, the cross is *the* symbol of deconstruction.

The gospels portray Jesus as so truthful that he lived this reality through to its inevitable conclusion: his own crucifixion. Paul developed and articulated the theology through to its logical conclusion: the rejection of him, his letters, his gospel and his Jesus by the earliest church.

The whole bible is permeated with this issue. Every writer wrestles with this perplexity. Why will every thought that exalts itself be pulled down? Why does the faith carry within it the seeds of its own destruction? Why must everything end up at Golgotha, there to be tried, tested, tortured and threatened with termination? Why is anything that is something menaced by nothingness? And why is only nothingness promised to be left alone and perhaps, in due time, exalted?

These are questions that harassed the biblical writers and should unsettle the church today.

Pastoral Integrity (January 26, 2011)

Pastors: if you don't own or have never read Eugene Peterson's excellent book, *Working the Angles: The Shape of Pastoral Integrity*, then you should buy it as soon as you can and add it to your arsenal of books. It belongs in every pastor's library. I bought it when it first came out: the year of my ordination, 1987. I read it every once in a while. In my opinion it should become a classic.

His three angles for pastoral integrity are:
1. prayer
2. scripture
3. spiritual direction

These are the three angles pastors should be experts in.

If I'm not mistaken, there is only one place in the entire book that he mentions vision:

> It is far less challenging to deliver a sermon than to develop the person who preaches it. It is far more stimulating to organize and administrate a parish program crisply than to live for weeks or months in uncertainty waiting patiently for clarity of vision.

I would dare say his idea of vision in no way resembles the visionary fervor in the church today. In fact, from the tone of the rest of his writings, such as when he expresses his appreciation for the American farmer and essayist Wendell Berry, one can only conclude that he advocates a far more pastoral ecclessiology than most would prefer today.

Vision Like Yeast (March 11, 2011)

If you want your church community life to be healthy, then keeping it free of vision, goals and purpose is a high priority.

This is how I spent most of my effort during my time in the professional ministry as a pastor. It took a great deal of discernment, courage and will from me and my team and others to make sure that our church community didn't sink into this terrible vortex of purpose-drivenness.

What I've discovered and conclude is that you can't expect to determine this at the beginning and forget about it, as if you've implemented an immutable unbreakable law that has set the character of your community in motion forever. It will be constantly challenged from the beginning. Like the victimization of grace upon which the law incessantly attempts to invade and encroach and replace... often successfully... likewise your community will be ceaselessly tempted to allow just a little

purpose, some kind of goal or a vision.

I promise you that one speck of this yeast will work its way through the whole batch of dough and change your community completely and forever. It will be practically impossible to go back. It will be as difficult to remove this infection as it would be to remove the yeast after the dough is risen.

Idolatry and the Sublimation of Self (May 2, 2011)

The root word of sublimation is sublime. It refers to the process of making something gross into something more sublime.

Scientifically, sublimation refers to the process of transition of a substance from the solid phase to the gas phase without passing through an intermediate liquid phase.

In **psychology**, sublimation is when socially unacceptable impulses are consciously transformed into socially acceptable behavior that serves a higher cultural or socially useful purpose.

I suggest that in **religion**, sublimation refers to the transformation of natural human impulses and needs into religious activities that serve the interests of the institution.

I recently had a conversation with a young man. I asked how he was doing. He said he was going through stuff right now but that he was all right. I invited him to share what he was going through. He had just been dismissed from the staff of a large church. He and his wife and children were shocked to discover that he was made redundant by the church leadership and was suddenly unemployed and in quite desperate shape financially and vocationally. I said something like, *"Wow!"* He countered, *"No, no! It's okay. I understand. I questioned some things. I guess the pastor figured I wasn't as on board as he wanted so he had me dismissed. Makes sense."* I felt angry for him. I had been through that kind of thing more than once, and I knew the pain of it very well. I told him, *"No way! That's not right. I'd be angry about that. I hate that when churches punish you for not being 100% with the program!"* We talked for quite a while. I don't think we parted in agreement.

This happens all the time. Not just to staff but to members. It has happened to me several times. So I know it must be happening many times a day.

This is **idolatry**. When you don't serve the idol in whatever shape it manifests itself, when you don't submit to it with complete and unquestioning loyalty, when you are not fully sold out to it, when you don't transform your natural human self into useful religious energy and activity, then you are rejected by the idol, its vision and its authorities. Religion sacrifices the human spirit and peoples' lives to its sublime agenda.

Whether this has its place in some corporations, businesses, organizations and institutions, is one thing. But it is counter-spiritual in the church because it is primarily against the human being. It is so prevalent in this world that when it happens in the church very few question it, even when they are direct victims of it. Rather than the church being a fellowship of sinners, normal human beings gathered in voluntary community, it has become the alchemical locus for cooking people into something more desirable, productive, fertile and useful to the religious program. And like all idols, it is hungry for more and more human flesh in order to consume it and transmute it into the security and promotion of its own life.

ABOUT THE AUTHOR

David Hayward lives near Saint John, New Brunswick, Canada, with his wife
Lisa. David was ordained and served the church as a pastor for over 25 years.
He teaches English as a Second Language to international students at Saint John
College, the University of New Brunswick, Saint John. David and Lisa have
three children. He also runs the blog, nakedpastor.com

©nakedpastor
nakedpastor®
All images belong to David Hayward.